A NOTE ABOUT DEMOCRACY:
A CIVICS PRIMER FOR THE 21ST CENTURY

By Jordan De La Sierra

❖ ❖ ❖

Prologue By Richard Lang

❖

A Note About Democracy

❖

*"Books give a soul to the universe,
wings to the mind,
flight to the imagination,
and life to everything."*

—Plato

*A NOTE ABOUT DEMOCRACY:
A CIVICS PRIMER FOR THE 21ST CENTURY*

By Jordan De La Sierra

❖ ❖ ❖

Prologue By Richard Lang

❖

Copyright © 2024 by Jordan De La Sierra
All Rights Reserved.

First Published in the United States of America in 2024 by
Amazon Publishing Agency.

For information about permission to reproduce selections from this book,
please address all correspondence to:
civicsphere101@gmail.com

Library of Congress Cataloging-in-Publication Data
Jordan De La Sierra.

A Note About Democracy: A Civics Primer For The 21st Century -
Written by Jordan De La Sierra.

ISBN: 978-1-963789-00-3
LCCN (Library of Congress control number): 2024901590

All future copyright renewals held in perpetuity by Jordan De La Sierra and
the De La Sierra Education Foundational Trust.

As life-long learners, we are an association of dedicated citizens committed
to bringing to life the lessons of civics to students of all ages.

Working together, free of animus toward anyone,
we strive to nurture and sustain a more just and egalitarian society.

Through the beneficent agency of education, we celebrate the gift of democracy.

To discover more, visit us at: civicsphere.life

*I wish to thank my artist friends, Richard and Judith Lang,
for encouraging me to send these thought-forms out into the world.*

*With gratitude to my dear friend, Hans Jacob Fossedahl,
whose endless curiosity and generosity of spirit has enlivened
our ongoing conversation for nigh unto fifty years.*

Contents:

Dedication and Acknowledgments .... *11.*

Prologue by Richard Lang .... *13.*

A Note About Democracy .... *17.*

Epilogue .... *27.*

About the Author .... *29.*

Addenda Contents .... *31.*

Addenda Part I.:   Founding Documents .... *33.*

Addenda Part II.:   Notable Speeches .... *57.*

Addenda Part III.:   Isonomia - A Brief Synopsis of An Ancient Idea .... *101.*

Addenda Part IV.:   Bibliography - Recommended Reading & More .... *103.*

Addenda V.:   Songs From The Nature House .... *119.*

x.

Dedication

To wit and to wisdom and the humor it affords.

*To my mother and my father
who raised me with an open mind
and set me on my course,
instilling in me, along the way,
an enduring love of nature.*

*To my treasured teachers
whose lessons never fade
and whose voices still ring clear.*

*To ev'ry man and ev'ry woman
who've inspired me on the way.*

To all who gave me shelter from the storm.

*To ev'ry child, from ev'rywhere
whose voices must be heard.*

*To my wife who,
ev'ryday in her own way,
makes the world a wee bit better place.*

"For there is but one essential justice which cements society, and one law which establishes this justice. This law is right reason, which is the true rule of all commandments and prohibitions. Whoever neglects this law, whether written or unwritten, is necessarily unjust and wicked."

—Marcus Tullius Cicero

Prologue:

Jordan De La Sierra's 'Note About Democracy' is offering youngsters of all ages a primer of great importance. In this age when we are silo-ed into thinking the thoughts our algorithmic masters want us to think, he is inviting us to consider new ways to explore our curiosity about things; new ways to expand our imaginations; new ways to think for ourselves.

As the advancing technology continues to catalog our every click-and-swipe, showing us, instant by instant, where we have been and what we last looked at, De La Sierra is asking us to take a minute to look at something else. He is encouraging us to more closely examine what it means to be an informed citizen; what it means to be engaged in the ongoing conversation; what it means to embrace, more fully, the responsibilities of citizenship in the melting pot of 21st century America.

In my 8th grade civics class, it was mandatory to study and pass an exam to be able to go on to high school. Our studies included a thorough review of the Illinois State Constitution and the Federal Constitution, as well. To complete our classwork, we were required to memorize the preamble to the U.S. Constitution:

We the People of the United States, in Order to form a more perfect Union, establish Justice, insure domestic Tranquility, provide for the common defence, promote the general Welfare, and secure the Blessings of Liberty to ourselves and our Posterity, do ordain and establish this Constitution for the United States of America.

Along with that, we were asked to commit to memory
the first paragraph of the Declaration of Independence:

We hold these truths to be self-evident, that all men are created equal,
that they are endowed by their Creator with certain unalienable Rights,
that among these are Life, Liberty and the pursuit of Happiness.

This was in 1960, sixty-two years ago at this writing.
Lots of water has passed under the bridge since then—the flood tide of the civil rights movement; the protests against the Vietnam War; the advent of 9/11; the Middle Eastern wars;
the Insurrection of January 6th and on and on and on.
Yet, after having faced it all, here we are still standing.

With the power of *We the People,* the cumbersome ship of state *can* gradually correct its course.
It is always *We the People* who are tasked with addressing our misguided choices.
It is always *We the people* who must face our fraught actions and deeds.
It is always *We the People* who must learn our hard-earned lessons.

Yes, it is always *We the People* who, though yet divided,
find ways to reach out, to pull together as one—
trimming the sails, seeing things through,
bringing the craft to safe harbor.

Now, our common purpose is a call for renewed civility,
a call to find the middle path, the path of truth and reason.
De La Sierra's essay is just the ticket—let's *We the People* keep
this great American experiment alive, shall we?

Richard Lang : 2022

"Wonder is the beginning of wisdom."

—Socrates

A NOTE ABOUT DEMOCRACY:

A CIVICS PRIMER FOR THE 21ˢᵗ CENTURY

Jordan De La Sierra / California / Winter 2021

Imagine, if you will, how hard it would be to take a group of wealthy European landowners, add in a diverse population of dirt-poor immigrants, a captive diaspora of African slaves, a conquered nation of indigenous peoples and a universe of women from everywhere with no right to own land and no right to vote and then, just like that, with all these strangely-juxtaposed, cultural-representatives cognitively engaged, start a debate.

Yes! With the audacity to attempt to blend these disparate human stories
into a common whole, the debate did indeed begin.

Imagine.

New world, new idea, new experiment. New democratic-republic here we come.

Having been born here and having spent their childhoods and their formative years embracing the ethos of the Renaissance and the Age of Reason, an inspired cohort of creative young men grew up on the shores of a virgin world. As precocious lads and inquisitive men,
they studied hard, gathering together to exchange ideas about the history of civilization
from the Egyptians to the Greeks to the Romans and beyond.

Avidly sharing thoughts and insights with one another,
their conversations delved into a wide array of subjects.
Along the way, they explored the time-honored fields
of mathematics and science, of philosophy and religion,
of the arts and the humanities; all this while keeping a close eye
on current events and the pressing issues of the day.

As members of an up and coming generation,
they were self-propelled; always willing to learn;
willing to evolve; willing to change and thrive.
Collectively, the trait they seemed to share the most
was their endless curiosity.

This is a note about what they did. This is a note about the birth of our democracy.

In the spirit of the Enlightenment, this band of friends and associates shared a common bond.
With unity of purpose, they were committed to establishing a new form of government.
They began a conversation that culminated in the convening of a convention. This convention,
this forum for the ages, was an assembly brought together to create the draft of an
operating system of sorts, a set of maps and models, an outline that included some
basic rules and essential laws, a time-capsule containing the spark of an idea,
a notion filled with endless possibilities, a kit-bag for the road.

Seemingly all at once, out of the blue, these highly intelligent, intellectually curious,
inveterate inventors, became the spark that lead to the drafting of the *Declaration of Independence*,
the drafting of a *Constitution* and the drafting of a *Bill of Rights*.

Starting from scratch, this group of founders launched a campaign to foster education.

Early on in their own evolution, these men had realized the importance and imperative of
universal learning. They saw education as an initiation into a process;
a life-long process of exploration, a process whose rewards are never-ending.

Educating the young, educating the old and all the folks in between
became an immutable priority, a prerequisite for all that was to follow.

Dedicated to their quintessential aim, this group of founders had to painstakingly
work to enlighten the lion's share of the population as to the ways in which democracies
are born and the ways in which they function.

When a population has never dealt with the responsibilities of citizenship in a democratically
organized system of self-government, it stands to reason that such a population will require
a practical primer in matters of civic engagement.

When a population has no idea of what it means to live in a society that honors the rule of law or
in a place where equal rights and justice are not only extolled as virtues but are, in word and in deed,
in fact, upheld; in a place where freedom of religion and freedom from religion are equally regarded
as rights to be respected; in a place where, in the name of sanity and rational discourse, a wall
separating matters of church and state stands as a sentinel protecting the rights of law-abiding
citizens of every stripe and inclination; in a place where civic education is the order of the day;
in a place where the ways and means of government are taught all across the land.

When a population has never lived in a thriving, self-governing democracy,
it is hard to imagine what the experience is like.

It is different from any of the many time-honored patriarchal or matriarchal forms of government
found scattered across the landscape of human history. It is different from governments
dominated by strict, sectarian, religious hierarchies. It is different from governing principles
practiced by nations of tribes and chiefs and elders whose indigenous roots celebrate a seamless
remembrance of their relationship with the living world. And, it is different from any authoritarian,
oligarchic, plutocratic, demagogic, fascistic or politically twisted, dictatorial model
of absolute power and unfettered control. Yes. Democracy is different.

Whether we are members of a city-state or nation mercilessly caught in the grips of anarchy;
whether we live in a country or in a world transitioning from chaos to dictatorship;
whether we live in a realm or in a kingdom transitioning from monarchy to aristocracy
or from aristocracy to democracy, the cycle keeps on spinning.

If and when, due to some beneficent circumstance, we are afforded an opportunity
to be or to become a citizen of a true democracy, a citizen willing to work to
sustain such an ever-evolving, ever-refining system of self-government, we must be
vigilant stewards of the enterprise. In this auspicious governing-model,
personal accountability is essential. Without question, exercising
good citizenship is the best way to nurture and to honor
such a shared, providential inheritance.

This commitment to harmoniously contributing to the well-being of the commonwealth and to all
that underpins a thriving social order is, in itself, a virtuous expression of ethical and moral integrity.

As it turns out, true democracy is not an arrival point. It's an aspiration. Generation after generation,
true democracy is forever an unfinished process. Often advancing incrementally,
often in fits and starts, it is, by its very nature, an endlessly, challenging task.

With persistent, painstaking effort, working to achieve some degree of consensus, new ideas are
proposed, new ideas are debated and, occasionally, new ideas find their way into law.
Slowly but surely, change arrives, rarely as fast as we'd like. But, in due course,
if all goes well, progress inches along.

In the journey toward a more just and egalitarian society, it is essential that elected leaders respond
appropriately to the needs and to the will of the people. Along with a dose of humility, a keen
sense of humanity is required. If one is to fulfill the constitutional responsibilities inherent in any
act of good governance, having a level head and a robust sense of humor doesn't hurt. However,
no matter how politically expedient it may appear to be at the time, no act of government should ever
be leveraged against or, in any way, brought to bear at the expense of the rule of law.

Even when the system is thriving, movement on new propositions proceeds at a veritable snail's pace.
At every juncture, things have the potential to undergo refinement. Yet, gradually, over the course
of time, things can and do improve, enriching the quality of life for all in ways that really count.

In the case of the United States of America, the fact that this democratic, governing model has
endured this long and advanced this far is truly a miracle of sorts; a transpiration of the first magnitude.
The flower of our democracy has just begun to bloom. It's only in the last 50 years or so,
that our experiment in government has reached the first stages of maturity.

From the birth of our republic until relatively recent times, our attempt, as a nation,
to establish and maintain a viable democracy has been heralded, in many quarters,
as 'the shot heard 'round the world'. In the pantheon of empires, nations,
nation-states and republics, our mercurial rise to power and influence
has proven to be an historically significant marker in
the compendium of human achievement.

Though we're not done yet, we, as a thriving democracy, are under threat.

No matter what our destiny, no matter how much longer this inspired experiment
can move forward and evolve is, as yet, an open question. Faced with our demise
as a true democracy, we're at a tipping point. If we fail to right the ship, history will
remember this moment. History will remember this juncture when a great democracy
was undermined, not so much by from forces without, but, more substantially, by forces from within.

As sad and catastrophic as it will be if the whole thing comes undone, this brief, meritorious effort
will not be soon forgotten. Historically, it will remain a signal example; an enduring
beacon to future generations; a lighthouse on the rocky shores of time.

In their dialogues, Plato and Aristotle thought the idea of true democracy was a noble aim,
but posited, by way of a warning, that the endeavor to establish such a democratic system
is fraught with pitfalls that work against its long-term sustainability.

From these masters of the forum, we learn how difficult it is to bring into being a functioning model
of any form of representative government. As we go forward, we heed their admonition when they
say that: 'on its way to becoming viable, such a system faces many hurdles'.
Of that there can be no doubt.

When a population has no idea of what it means to have the right to vote and has never lived
or thrived in any kind of democratically-inspired republic whose self-attenuating philosophy
is representative government, it is difficult for that population to imagine how such a system
could come to be. And, if it did come to be, how would the whole thing work?

Since the year 1789, we as citizens and we as immigrants aspiring to become citizens, must discover
for ourselves that such a framework of governance does, in fact, exist and, because it exists,
imperfect as it is, it gives us the right to explore what it means to live in a country that
continues to honor its cornerstone idea: the notion that, together as one, we are
'a government of, a government by and a government for the people'.

When this realization begins to dawn on folks, it's a moment to remember.
It's monumental. It's a really, really, really big deal.

Looking back to where the whole thing began, we can only imagine some of the physical
environments where the founders of our nation first broached their proposition. As they
traveled the back roads and haunted the hillsides, holding forth in the inns and the taverns,
convening in churches and halls, they boldly expressed their intentions. With growing confidence,
they conveyed their visionary plans to an ever widening audience of sympathetic listeners.

When their nascent endeavor reached critical mass, they began to host public meetings, heralding,
for all to hear, their purpose and their aim. Breathing the air of the commons, they congregated
openly, unabashedly addressing friend and foe alike. Consistently, with patience and precision, they
outlined their ideas about the 'great idea', exploring the 'noble experiment' from many points of view.
'To establish a new form of government' was the mission that drove them on. And, to that end, they
remained steadfast, articulate emissaries, unwavering in their dedication to that daunting quest.

We can only wonder how they framed
their initial arguments to the folks in the public square?

Did they perhaps begin by saying something of this nature?

"Greetings, one and all. Friends and acquaintances, rich and poor alike,
strangers in our midst, allies and foes, as well. Welcome.
Welcome to the speakers. Welcome to the listeners.
Welcome to the greater conversation."

"From the start, we have to confess our humanness, our temporal limitations.
We don't know even a thimble full about a lot of things,
but, little by little, together we learn a wee bit more each day."

"There's a lot to cover, here. Where do we begin?"

"This is a conversation about an ancient idea, an idea rarely explored,
an idea called democracy. At its essence, its far-reaching consequence
is the seed at the heart of our quest to achieve a new form of responsible government.
Today, we'll address the pros and cons, the virtues and drawbacks inherent
in the system we propose."

At the outset of the interaction, someone might stand up and ask:

"What are the conscientious acts that could contribute
to the success or failure of such a bold endeavor?"

"Good question", is the moderator's candid response. "Your inquiry is very cogent.
There are many challenges ahead, many choices left to make.
We'll address your keen insights and points forthwith."

Another attendee might inquire:

"Out of respect for this idea of democracy, out of respect for this idea of creating a new, self-
governing republic, will you take us through the the nuts-and-bolts of how such a system works?"

I posit that the foregoing, hypothetical play within a play - the narrative greeting;
the statement of purpose; the subsequent, follow-up dialogues; the questions and answers; all -
is meant to convey a sense of a moment in time; a snapshot reflection, a read out of sorts
depicting events as they very well may have occurred.

Convening and re-convening, meeting for sometimes days on end, these conversations
continued as the ideas that they pondered gradually took hold.

To breathe life into such a democratically-civilized society,
folks of every stripe and every unique persuasion need to acquire and
demonstrate a fundamental awareness of public life in townships,
in cities, in states, in nations and in planetary affairs.

This is the stuff that democracies are made of.

When people from all walks of life embrace the responsibilities
of citizenship in a democratic republic, the democracy flourishes.

With a veritable operating manual, a Constitution and a Bill of Rights
and, with a willingness to embrace any constructive amendment that can lead
to the furtherance of the common good, one could say the experiment is always beginning.

When citizens deny the vote, betray the truth and foster violent means,
the young democratic experiment begins to unravel. In such an environment, the virtues of reason,
rational discourse and equality under law fall prey to anarchistic factions and autocratic spells.

In a land where settlers of European extraction conquered the Americas
from sea-to-shining-sea, scooping up the spoils of war as they made their blood-soaked way.
In a land where tribe after tribe of native peoples were assaulted, maimed and killed,
their cultures and their way of life uprooted and destroyed. In a land where, in fact,
an unacknowledged genocide took place. In a land where the slave-trade came rushing in
to cultivate the humid, southern climes. In a land where plantations sprouted up like weeds
all along Tobacco Road. In a land where sugar cane and cotton paved the way to civil war.
In a land where re-construction failed and the 'lost cause' lumbered on. In a land where
robber-barons ruled the roost and the gilded age was born. In a land where women fought for
and secured their long-sought right to vote. In a land where child labor laws were painstakingly
enacted and universally enforced. In a land that sent its sons to fight and die abroad in WWI.
In a land where the 'Great Depression' brought the country to its knees. In a land where,
against a tide of fear and greed, the 'New Deal' instilled hope, serving, stumbling, striving on,
addressing many wrongs. In a land that sacrificed its sons and daughters fighting WWII. In a land
where unions thrived and workers' rights, for a time, took center stage. In a land where our leaders
convened to create the Marshall Plan to aid in the re-construction of Western Europe at the end
of WWII. In a land that worked with countries all around the world to foster the establishment of the
United Nations as an international forum for dialogue. In a land where President Eisenhower
helped to shepherd in the construction of the Interstate Freeway System. In a land where that same
U.S. President, speaking on his way out the door, shared with us the warning that we all must be
cognizant of the perils inherent in the opaque super-structure of the Military-Industrial Complex.
In a land where the 'Voting Rights Act' of 1965 was finally enacted and signed into law.
In a land where the 'Great Society', resented by some, advanced, for a time, a new
measure of justice and equality. In a land that was able to put a man on the moon
and safely return from the journey – seeing Earth from the moon,
a spinning, blue orb, this planet, a world like no other.

Looking forward, we see a growing host of issues, all waiting to be dealt with
and resolved. We don't know if or when these pressing matters will one day be addressed,
but, here and now, we do know what some of these issues are. For example: In the year 2022,
we live in a land where voting rights are being universally undermined. Taking advantage of a
simple majority, Republican legislatures, in state after state, are steadily disenfranchising millions
and millions of voters, worthy citizens all - racial minorities, college students, the elderly,
the immobilized and the infirm. We live in a land where a Senate rule, to wit: the filibuster,
is often deployed in diabolical ways to thwart conscientious debate, delaying, blocking, suspending
attempts to enact fair and just legislation. We live in a land where the archaic concept and influence
of an Electoral College has fostered the on-going imposition of sustained, minority rule. We live
in a land where big oil holds the upper hand and fossil fuels are king. We live in a land where the
unchecked proliferation of plastic generation and plastic waste threatens the life of all living things.
We live in a land where catastrophes caused by climate change can no longer be denied. We live
in a land where the restoration, maintenance and modernization of our nation's infrastructure has,
for far too long, gone substantially unaddressed. We live in a land where once, not so long ago,
the richest of the rich paid their rightful share of state and federal taxes. We live in a land where
robbery by gun; murder by gun; mass-shooting by gun and, suicide by gun, occur everywhere and
all the time at a most alarming rate. We live in a land where the manufacture and wide-spread
distribution of semi-automatic pistols and long guns and the ammo they employ, continue to sell
at a manic pace as if there were no tomorrow. We live in a land where the Supreme Court,
once a peerless bastion of solemn jurisprudence has, to its detriment and ultimate disgrace,
devolved into a quasi-political forum bent on the advancement of transparently, partisan ends.
We live in a land where deficit-hawks and anti-tax crusaders have ceaselessly campaigned
against federal support of almost every social program and public works, writ large. We live
in a land where 'culture wars' have taken center stage. We live in a land where
open-carry laws continue to be enacted in states around the country, allowing
who-knows-who to bring their deadly weapons into the public square.

Over the last 234 years, our democracy has endured many ups and downs and, through it all,
our institutions have survived. The center has held. The legislative, judicial and executive
branches of the tree have stayed strong and independent. As imperfect as we've been
as a nation, we've continued to make strides to improve the greater commonwealth
and promote the public good.

In recent times, however, there has been a gradual erosion of civility and rational discourse.
Our national conversation has become more and more fraught with conflict.
Not since the Civil War has our system of government
faced a challenge of this magnitude.

As of late, coming from within and fostered from without, anarchistic sympathizers and
paramilitary cells exacerbate divisions in our country.

Bigotry in camouflage is hiding in plain sight.
Wrapped in the robes of religion, purveying, still,
the fearsome emblems of the modern Ku Klux Klan,
white nationalists foment racism, xenophobia and hate as they
proselytize irrational conspiracies, engaging more and more overtly in massive acts of violence.

Day and night, utilizing social media as their platforms of choice,
autocratic opportunists swoop in to exploit the situation in any way they can,
gathering like scavengers ready to pick the carcass clean.

And now, the 'Big Lie', spread by the 'Great Pretender' and his acolytes,
blazes like a raging fire through the body politic. The justly and utterly
defeated, former president, continues his quest to avenge his loss as he
masquerades as the 'Anointed One', destroying in his wake whatever
remains standing in opposition to his willful nature.

While one of our political parties stands in silent acquiescence
as the madness of the clown car races by,
the structures of our democracy are under stress.
Cracks are appearing in the foundation.
Key elements of the experiment are
beginning to give way.

This is a time like no other, a time to put partisanship and politics aside;
a time for citizens of every stripe to pull for country over party.
No more red-state-this and blue-state that, no, that stuff's got to go.

Let's join in common cause.

In this hour of division and despair; in this hour of our existential angst,
let's honor the banner that unites us. Let's honor our priceless Constitution.
Let's re-double our effort to preserve this rarely attempted,
rarely sustained, model of self-government.

Let's breathe new life into this inspired, democratic republic, this country that we love.

We still have the requisite elements and fundamental
structures in place to survive the present challenge.
The only thing is, we, as citizens, have to have the will,
individually and collectively, to face the crisis at hand.

Unencumbered access to the ballot is the over-arching issue of the day.

Now is the hour, the moment to act is at hand.
This is the time to double-down and be vigilant.
Such a finely balanced system of government can easily slip away.

You know and I know, we can do better than this.
Let's save our treasured democracy from the vicissitudes of chaos and oblivion.

With an eye to justice and equality under law;
with an eye to the health and well-being of all citizens,
let's continue our work as we strive to achieve a more sound and more perfect union.

Please note: The following quotation was taken from an interview between presidential historian, Jon Meacham and news journalist, Brian Williams, aired on MSNBC's
'The 11th Hour' on Friday, 19 June 2021.

As Mr. Meacham posited so well in his recent conversation, and I paraphrase:

*"In American democracy there are no fairy-tale, once-upon-a-time beginnings
and no happily-ever-after endings. As a country, as a nation, we remain a work in progress."*

As I complete my note, I leave you with this thought.

Maintaining a great democracy is not unlike maintaining a great garden.
In order for each to flourish, vigilance and conscientious work are required.

As with all living things in our care, constant nurture and
lasting dedication are key to bringing forth the best results.

In this hour that threatens to undermine the pillars of our democracy,
let's protect this up-and-coming sprout, this fragile blossom.

As the sound of freedom's bell still rings and echoes 'round the world,
let's breathe new life into this rare experiment.

Let's surprise ourselves. Let's choose to pull together.
Just imagine all the good we can accomplish.
Imagine all the great things we can do.

Come on.
Let's get after it.
What are we waiting for?

*"A gem cannot be polished without friction,
nor a man perfected without trials."*

—Seneca

Author's Note – An Epilogue:

To Wit:

Are we tomorrow's utopian nomads, makers and traders of the tools of the future –
beacons whose bright, isonomian ethos sheds light on democracy's unfinished quest –
inspiring, uplifting and bringing to life a more just and more equitable world?

Or:

Are we, per chance, more like Anarchy's children who, faced with extinction,
rise up from the ashes – engaging, undoing, averting, at last,
the spell of oblivion's chaos and the rush to our certain demise?

Will we learn as we go, as we find ourselves scanning the vast, dry horizon
in search of a safe drink of water or a cave with more breathable air?

After all the destruction, what will we see? What we will we hear?
What will we sense in that great, silent void?

Over yonder, beyond that still, still mythic, Boot Hill,
what will we find in the relics and remnants?
What will we find, there, in old Tombstone town?

What will we glean that might give us a glimpse
into where we once traveled and who we once were?

Postscript:

On January 19th 2023, the Philadelphia Inquirer posted an editorial
with the headline *'Functioning Democracy Needs Media Literacy'*.

As I read the editorial, I was delighted to find that the State of New Jersey
has chosen to become the first state in the union to require schools to
teach media literacy to K-12 students.

Once implemented, this far-reaching decision has the potential to educate
this generation and future generations as to the true impact and real-world
consequences of social media's tacit complicity in the spread of lies,
half-truths, conspiracy theories and all manner of misinformation
and disinformation throughout the body politic and all
around this sacred, living planet that we love.

Kudos to New Jersey.

Let's hope that every state in the union will follow New Jersey's lead.

"The journey is the thing."

—Homer

About The Author

Mr. De La Sierra is a free-thinking, creative person.
Always curious and willing to learn, always given to invention,
he is best known for his work in art, his work in music and his work in poetry.

Throughout his journey, he has remained true to his life-long
exploration of practical solutions and beautiful ideas.

Here, as he addresses a wide spectrum of issues critical to the
survival and sustenance of a thriving democracy, he remains
focused on the state of the nation's general welfare
and the well-being of humanity as a whole.

His authority, his gravitas, derives from years and years of disciplined practice,
a practice evidenced in the renaissance-like breadth and quality
of his many artistic achievements.

Addenda Contents

Part I.: Founding Documents

  Declaration of Independence
  U.S. Constitution
  Bill of Rights

Part II.: Notable Speeches

  George Washington Farewell Address
  Abraham Lincoln Gettysburg Address
  Abraham Lincoln Second Inaugural Address
  Franklin Delano Roosevelt's Renomination Acceptance Speech / 1936 Democratic Convention
  Dwight D. Eisenhower's Farewell Address
  John F. Kennedy's Inaugural Address
  Martin Luther King, Jr.'s 'I Have A Dream Speech' / 28 August 1963
  Barack Obama's Keynote Address at the 2004 Democratic National Convention

Part III.: Isonomia: A Brief Synopsis of An Ancient Idea

Part IV.: A Bibliography With On-Line Links and References

  Richard Lang's Recommended Reading
  Jordan De La Sierra's Recommended Reading
  Jordan De La Sierra's Recommended Listening
  Jordan De La Sierra's Recommended Viewing

Part V.: 'Songs From the Nature House'

In this last entry, readers will find a small selection
of poems, hymns and literary confessions taken
from a trove of my collected writings.

Each of the pieces I've chosen to include
reflect an aspect of the creative ethos
at the heart of my life and work.

Addenda Part I.: Founding Documents

Declaration of Independence

WHEN in the Course of human Events, it becomes necessary for one People to dissolve the Political Bands which have connected them with another, and to assume among the Powers of the Earth, the separate and equal Station to which the Laws of Nature and of Nature's God entitle them, a decent Respect to the Opinions of Mankind requires that they should declare the causes which impel them to the Separation.

We hold these Truths to be self-evident, that all Men are created equal, that they are endowed by their Creator with certain unalienable Rights, that among these are Life, Liberty, and the Pursuit of Happiness—-That to secure these Rights, Governments are instituted among Men, deriving their just Powers from the Consent of the Governed, that whenever any Form of Government becomes destructive of these Ends, it is the Right of the People to alter or to abolish it, and to institute new Government, laying its Foundation on such Principles, and organizing its Powers in such Form, as to them shall seem most likely to effect their Safety and Happiness. Prudence, indeed, will dictate that Governments long established should not be changed for light and transient Causes; and accordingly all Experience hath shewn, that Mankind are more disposed to suffer, while Evils are sufferable, than to right themselves by abolishing the Forms to which they are accustomed. But when a long Train of Abuses and Usurpations, pursuing invariably the same Object, evinces a Design to reduce them under absolute Despotism, it is their Right, it is their Duty, to throw off such Government, and to provide new Guards for their future Security. Such has been the patient Sufferance of these Colonies; and such is now the Necessity which constrains them to alter their former Systems of Government. The History of the present King of Great-Britain is a History of repeated Injuries and Usurpations, all having in direct Object the Establishment of an absolute Tyranny over these States. To prove this, let Facts be submitted to a candid World.

He has refused his Assent to Laws, the most wholesome and necessary for the public Good.

He has forbidden his Governors to pass Laws of immediate and pressing Importance, unless suspended in their Operation till his Assent should be obtained; and when so suspended, he has utterly neglected to attend to them.

He has refused to pass other Laws for the Accommodation of large Districts of People, unless those People would relinquish the Right of Representation in the Legislature, a Right inestimable to them, and formidable to Tyrants only.

He has called together Legislative Bodies at Places unusual, uncomfortable, and distant from the Depository of their public Records, for the sole Purpose of fatiguing them into Compliance with his Measures.

He has dissolved Representative Houses repeatedly, for opposing with manly Firmness his Invasions on the Rights of the People.

He has refused for a long Time, after such Dissolutions, to cause others to be elected; whereby the Legislative Powers, incapable of Annihilation, have returned to the People at large for their exercise; the State remaining in the mean time exposed to all the Dangers of Invasion from without, and Convulsions within.

He has endeavoured to prevent the Population of these States; for that Purpose obstructing the Laws for Naturalization of Foreigners; refusing to pass others to encourage their Migrations hither, and raising the Conditions of new Appropriations of Lands.

He has obstructed the Administration of Justice, by refusing his Assent to Laws for establishing Judiciary Powers.

He has made Judges dependent on his Will alone, for the Tenure of their Offices, and the Amount and Payment of their Salaries.

He has erected a Multitude of new Offices, and sent hither Swarms of Officers to harass our People, and eat out their Substance.

He has kept among us, in Times of Peace, Standing Armies, without the consent of our Legislatures.

He has affected to render the Military independent of and superior to the Civil Power.

He has combined with others to subject us to a Jurisdiction foreign to our Constitution, and unacknowledged by our Laws; giving his Assent to their Acts of pretended Legislation:

For quartering large Bodies of Armed Troops among us:

For protecting them, by a mock Trial, from Punishment for any Murders which they should commit on the Inhabitants of these States:

For cutting off our Trade with all Parts of the World:

For imposing Taxes on us without our Consent:

For depriving us, in many Cases, of the Benefits of Trial by Jury:

For transporting us beyond Seas to be tried for pretended Offences:

For abolishing the free System of English Laws in a neighbouring Province, establishing therein an arbitrary Government, and enlarging its Boundaries, so as to render it at once an Example and fit Instrument for introducing the same absolute Rule into these Colonies:

For taking away our Charters, abolishing our most valuable Laws, and altering fundamentally the Forms of our Governments:

For suspending our own Legislatures, and declaring themselves invested with Power to legislate for us in all Cases whatsoever.

He has abdicated Government here, by declaring us out of his Protection and waging War against us.

He has plundered our Seas, ravaged our Coasts, burnt our Towns, and destroyed the Lives of our People.

He is, at this Time, transporting large Armies of foreign Mercenaries to complete the Works of Death, Desolation, and Tyranny, already begun with circumstances of Cruelty and Perfidy, scarcely paralleled in the most barbarous Ages, and totally unworthy the Head of a civilized Nation.

He has constrained our fellow Citizens taken Captive on the high Seas to bear Arms against their Country, to become the Executioners of their Friends and Brethren, or to fall themselves by their Hands.

He has excited domestic Insurrections amongst us, and has endeavoured to bring on the Inhabitants of our Frontiers, the merciless Indian Savages, whose known Rule of Warfare, is an undistinguished Destruction, of all Ages, Sexes and Conditions.

In every stage of these Oppressions we have Petitioned for Redress in the most humble Terms: Our repeated Petitions have been answered only by repeated Injury. A Prince, whose Character is thus marked by every act which may define a Tyrant, is unfit to be the Ruler of a free People.

Nor have we been wanting in Attentions to our British Brethren. We have warned them from Time to Time of Attempts by their Legislature to extend an unwarrantable Jurisdiction over us. We have reminded them of the Circumstances of our Emigration and Settlement here. We have appealed to their native Justice and Magnanimity, and we have conjured them by the Ties of our common Kindred to disavow these Usurpations, which, would inevitably interrupt our Connections and Correspondence. They too have been deaf to the Voice of Justice and of Consanguinity. We must, therefore, acquiesce in the Necessity, which denounces our Separation, and hold them, as we hold the rest of Mankind, Enemies in War, in Peace, Friends.

We, therefore, the Representatives of the UNITED STATES OF AMERICA, in General Congress, Assembled, appealing to the Supreme Judge of the World for the Rectitude of our Intentions, do, in the Name, and by Authority of the good People of these Colonies, solemnly Publish and Declare, That these United Colonies are, and of Right ought to be, Free and Independent States; that they are absolved from all Allegiance to the British Crown, and that all political Connection between them and the State of Great-Britain, is and ought to be totally dissolved; and that as Free and Independent States, they have full Power to levy War, conclude Peace, contract Alliances, establish Commerce, and to do all other Acts and Things which Independent States may of right do. And for the support of this Declaration, with a firm Reliance on the Protection of divine Providence, we mutually pledge to each other our Lives, our Fortunes, and our sacred Honor.

Signed by Order and in Behalf of the Congress,
JOHN HANCOCK, President.

Attest.
CHARLES THOMSON, Secretary.

United States Constitution

We the People of the United States, in Order to form a more perfect Union, establish Justice, insure domestic Tranquility, provide for the common defence, promote the general Welfare, and secure the Blessings of Liberty to ourselves and our Posterity, do ordain and establish this Constitution for the United States of America.

Article. I.

Section. 1.

All legislative Powers herein granted shall be vested in a Congress of the United States, which shall consist of a Senate and House of Representatives.

Section. 2.

The House of Representatives shall be composed of Members chosen every second Year by the People of the several States, and the Electors in each State shall have the Qualifications requisite for Electors of the most numerous Branch of the State Legislature.

No Person shall be a Representative who shall not have attained to the Age of twenty five Years, and been seven Years a Citizen of the United States, and who shall not, when elected, be an Inhabitant of that State in which he shall be chosen.

Representatives and direct Taxes shall be apportioned among the several States which may be included within this Union, according to their respective Numbers, which shall be determined by adding to the whole Number of free Persons, including those bound to Service for a Term of Years, and excluding Indians not taxed, three fifths of all other Persons. The actual Enumeration shall be made within three Years after the first Meeting of the Congress of the United States, and within every subsequent Term of ten Years, in such Manner as they shall by Law direct. The Number of Representatives shall not exceed one for every thirty Thousand, but each State shall have at Least one Representative; and until such enumeration shall be made, the State of New Hampshire shall be entitled to chuse three, Massachusetts eight, Rhode-Island and Providence Plantations one, Connecticut five, New-York six, New Jersey four, Pennsylvania eight, Delaware one, Maryland six, Virginia ten, North Carolina five, South Carolina five, and Georgia three.

When vacancies happen in the Representation from any State, the Executive Authority thereof shall issue Writs of Election to fill such Vacancies.

The House of Representatives shall chuse their Speaker and other Officers; and shall have the sole Power of Impeachment.

Section. 3.

The Senate of the United States shall be composed of two Senators from each State, chosen by the Legislature thereof, for six Years; and each Senator shall have one Vote.

Immediately after they shall be assembled in Consequence of the first Election, they shall be divided as equally as may be into three Classes.

The Seats of the Senators of the first Class shall be vacated at the Expiration of the second Year, of the second Class at the Expiration of the fourth Year, and of the third Class at the Expiration of the sixth Year, so that one third may be chosen every second Year; and if Vacancies happen by Resignation, or otherwise, during the Recess of the Legislature of any State, the Executive thereof may make temporary Appointments until the next Meeting of the Legislature, which shall then fill such Vacancies.

No Person shall be a Senator who shall not have attained to the Age of thirty Years, and been nine Years a Citizen of the United States, and who shall not, when elected, be an Inhabitant of that State for which he shall be chosen.

The Vice President of the United States shall be President of the Senate, but shall have no Vote, unless they be equally divided.

The Senate shall chuse their other Officers, and also a President pro tempore, in the Absence of the Vice President, or when he shall exercise the Office of President of the United States.

The Senate shall have the sole Power to try all Impeachments. When sitting for that Purpose, they shall be on Oath or Affirmation. When the President of the United States is tried, the Chief Justice shall preside: And no Person shall be convicted without the Concurrence of two thirds of the Members present.

Judgment in Cases of Impeachment shall not extend further than to removal from Office, and disqualification to hold and enjoy any Office of honor, Trust or Profit under the United States: but the Party convicted shall nevertheless be liable and subject to Indictment, Trial, Judgment and Punishment, according to Law.

Section. 4.

The Times, Places and Manner of holding Elections for Senators and Representatives, shall be prescribed in each State by the Legislature thereof; but the Congress may at any time by Law make or alter such Regulations, except as to the Places of chusing Senators.

The Congress shall assemble at least once in every Year, and such Meeting shall be on the first Monday in December, unless they shall by Law appoint a different Day.

Section. 5.

Each House shall be the Judge of the Elections, Returns and Qualifications of its own Members, and a Majority of each shall constitute a Quorum to do Business; but a smaller Number may adjourn from day to day, and may be authorized to compel the Attendance of absent Members, in such Manner, and under such Penalties as each House may provide.

Each House may determine the Rules of its Proceedings, punish its Members for disorderly Behaviour, and, with the Concurrence of two thirds, expel a Member.

Each House shall keep a Journal of its Proceedings, and from time to time publish the same, excepting such Parts as may in their Judgment require Secrecy; and the Yeas and Nays of the Members of either House on any question shall, at the Desire of one fifth of those Present, be entered on the Journal.

Neither House, during the Session of Congress, shall, without the Consent of the other, adjourn for more than three days, nor to any other Place than that in which the two Houses shall be sitting.

Section. 6.

The Senators and Representatives shall receive a Compensation for their Services, to be ascertained by Law, and paid out of the Treasury of the United States. They shall in all Cases, except Treason, Felony and Breach of the Peace, be privileged from Arrest during their Attendance at the Session of their respective Houses, and in going to and returning from the same; and for any Speech or Debate in either House, they shall not be questioned in any other Place.

No Senator or Representative shall, during the Time for which he was elected, be appointed to any civil Office under the Authority of the United States, which shall have been created, or the Emoluments whereof shall have been encreased during such time; and no Person holding any Office under the United States, shall be a Member of either House during his Continuance in Office.

Section. 7.

All Bills for raising Revenue shall originate in the House of Representatives; but the Senate may propose or concur with Amendments as on other Bills.

Every Bill which shall have passed the House of Representatives and the Senate, shall, before it become a Law, be presented to the President of the United States; If he approve he shall sign it, but if not he shall return it, with his Objections to that House in which it shall have originated, who shall enter the Objections at large on their Journal, and proceed to reconsider it. If after such Reconsideration two thirds of that House shall agree to pass the Bill, it shall be sent, together with the Objections, to the other House, by which it shall likewise be reconsidered, and if approved by two thirds of that House, it shall become a Law. But in all such Cases the Votes of both Houses shall be determined by yeas and Nays, and the Names of the Persons voting for and against the Bill shall be entered on the Journal of each House respectively. If any Bill shall not be returned by the President within ten Days (Sundays excepted) after it shall have been presented to him, the Same shall be a Law, in like Manner as if he had signed it, unless the Congress by their Adjournment prevent its Return, in which Case it shall not be a Law.

Every Order, Resolution, or Vote to which the Concurrence of the Senate and House of Representatives may be necessary (except on a question of Adjournment) shall be presented to the President of the United States; and before the Same shall take Effect, shall be approved by him, or being disapproved by him, shall be repassed by two thirds of the Senate and House of Representatives, according to the Rules and Limitations prescribed in the Case of a Bill.

Section. 8.

The Congress shall have Power To lay and collect Taxes, Duties, Imposts and Excises, to pay the Debts and provide for the common Defence and general Welfare of the United States; but all Duties, Imposts and Excises shall be uniform throughout the United States;

To borrow Money on the credit of the United States;

To regulate Commerce with foreign Nations, and among the several States, and with the Indian Tribes;

To establish an uniform Rule of Naturalization, and uniform Laws on the subject of Bankruptcies throughout the United States;

To coin Money, regulate the Value thereof, and of foreign Coin, and fix the Standard of Weights and Measures;

To provide for the Punishment of counterfeiting the Securities and current Coin of the United States;

To establish Post Offices and post Roads;

To promote the Progress of Science and useful Arts, by securing for limited Times to Authors and Inventors the exclusive Right to their respective Writings and Discoveries;

To constitute Tribunals inferior to the supreme Court;

To define and punish Piracies and Felonies committed on the high Seas, and Offences against the Law of Nations;

To declare War, grant Letters of Marque and Reprisal, and make Rules concerning Captures on Land and Water;

To raise and support Armies, but no Appropriation of Money to that Use shall be for a longer Term than two Years;

To provide and maintain a Navy;

To make Rules for the Government and Regulation of the land and naval Forces;

To provide for calling forth the Militia to execute the Laws of the Union, suppress Insurrections and repel Invasions;

To provide for organizing, arming, and disciplining, the Militia, and for governing such Part of them as may be employed in the Service of the United States, reserving to the States respectively, the Appointment of the Officers, and the Authority of training the Militia according to the discipline prescribed by Congress;

To exercise exclusive Legislation in all Cases whatsoever, over such District (not exceeding ten Miles square) as may, by Cession of particular States, and the Acceptance of Congress, become the Seat of the Government of the United States, and to exercise like Authority over all Places purchased by the Consent of the Legislature of the State in which the Same shall be, for the Erection of Forts, Magazines, Arsenals, dock-Yards, and other needful Buildings;—And

To make all Laws which shall be necessary and proper for carrying into Execution the foregoing Powers, and all other Powers vested by this Constitution in the Government of the United States, or in any Department or Officer thereof.

Section. 9.

The Migration or Importation of such Persons as any of the States now existing shall think proper to admit, shall not be prohibited by the Congress prior to the Year one thousand eight hundred and eight, but a Tax or duty may be imposed on such Importation, not exceeding ten dollars for each Person.

The Privilege of the Writ of Habeas Corpus shall not be suspended, unless when in Cases of Rebellion or Invasion the public Safety may require it.

No Bill of Attainder or ex post facto Law shall be passed.

No Capitation, or other direct, Tax shall be laid, unless in Proportion to the Census or enumeration herein before directed to be taken.

No Tax or Duty shall be laid on Articles exported from any State.

No Preference shall be given by any Regulation of Commerce or Revenue to the Ports of one State over those of another: nor shall Vessels bound to, or from, one State, be obliged to enter, clear, or pay Duties in another.

No Money shall be drawn from the Treasury, but in Consequence of Appropriations made by Law; and a regular Statement and Account of the Receipts and Expenditures of all public Money shall be published from time to time.

No Title of Nobility shall be granted by the United States: And no Person holding any Office of Profit or Trust under them, shall, without the Consent of the Congress, accept of any present, Emolument, Office, or Title, of any kind whatever, from any King, Prince, or foreign State.

Section. 10.

No State shall enter into any Treaty, Alliance, or Confederation; grant Letters of Marque and Reprisal; coin Money; emit Bills of Credit; make any Thing but gold and silver Coin a Tender in Payment of Debts; pass any Bill of Attainder, ex post facto Law, or Law impairing the Obligation of Contracts, or grant any Title of Nobility.

No State shall, without the Consent of the Congress, lay any Imposts or Duties on Imports or Exports, except what may be absolutely necessary for executing it's inspection Laws: and the net Produce of all Duties and Imposts, laid by any State on Imports or Exports, shall be for the Use of the Treasury of the United States; and all such Laws shall be subject to the Revision and Controul of the Congress.

No State shall, without the Consent of Congress, lay any Duty of Tonnage, keep Troops, or Ships of War in time of Peace, enter into any Agreement or Compact with another State, or with a foreign Power, or engage in War, unless actually invaded, or in such imminent Danger as will not admit of delay.

Article. II.

Section. 1.

The executive Power shall be vested in a President of the United States of America. He shall hold his Office during the Term of four Years, and, together with the Vice President, chosen for the same Term, be elected, as follows

Each State shall appoint, in such Manner as the Legislature thereof may direct, a Number of Electors, equal to the whole Number of Senators and Representatives to which the State may be entitled in the Congress: but no Senator or Representative, or Person holding an Office of Trust or Profit under the United States, shall be appointed an Elector.

The Electors shall meet in their respective States, and vote by Ballot for two Persons, of whom one at least shall not be an Inhabitant of the same State with themselves. And they shall make a List of all the Persons voted for, and of the Number of Votes for each; which List they shall sign and certify, and transmit sealed to the Seat of the Government of the United States, directed to the President of the Senate. The President of the Senate shall, in the Presence of the Senate and House of Representatives, open all the Certificates, and the Votes shall then be counted.

The Person having the greatest Number of Votes shall be the President, if such Number be a Majority of the whole Number of Electors appointed; and if there be more than one who have such Majority, and have an equal Number of Votes, then the House of Representatives shall immediately chuse by Ballot one of them for President; and if no Person have a Majority, then from the five highest on the List the said House shall in like Manner chuse the President. But in chusing the President, the Votes shall be taken by States, the Representation from each State having one Vote; A quorum for this Purpose shall consist of a Member or Members from two thirds of the States, and a Majority of all the States shall be necessary to a Choice. In every Case, after the Choice of the President, the Person having the greatest Number of Votes of the Electors shall be the Vice President. But if there should remain two or more who have equal Votes, the Senate shall chuse from them by Ballot the Vice President.

The Congress may determine the Time of chusing the Electors, and the Day on which they shall give their Votes; which Day shall be the same throughout the United States.

No Person except a natural born Citizen, or a Citizen of the United States, at the time of the Adoption of this Constitution, shall be eligible to the Office of President; neither shall any Person be eligible to that Office who shall not have attained to the Age of thirty five Years, and been fourteen Years a Resident within the United States.

In Case of the Removal of the President from Office, or of his Death, Resignation, or Inability to discharge the Powers and Duties of the said Office, the Same shall devolve on the Vice President, and the Congress may by Law provide for the Case of Removal, Death, Resignation or Inability, both of the President and Vice President, declaring what Officer shall then act as President, and such Officer shall act accordingly, until the Disability be removed, or a President shall be elected.

The President shall, at stated Times, receive for his Services, a Compensation, which shall neither be encreased nor diminished during the Period for which he shall have been elected, and he shall not receive within that Period any other Emolument from the United States, or any of them.

Before he enter on the Execution of his Office, he shall take the following Oath or Affirmation:—"I do solemnly swear (or affirm) that I will faithfully execute the Office of President of the United States, and will to the best of my Ability, preserve, protect and defend the Constitution of the United States."

Section. 2.

The President shall be Commander in Chief of the Army and Navy of the United States, and of the Militia of the several States, when called into the actual Service of the United States; he may require the Opinion, in writing, of the principal Officer in each of the executive Departments, upon any Subject relating to the Duties of their respective Offices, and he shall have Power to grant Reprieves and Pardons for Offences against the United States, except in Cases of Impeachment.

He shall have Power, by and with the Advice and Consent of the Senate, to make Treaties, provided two thirds of the Senators present concur; and he shall nominate, and by and with the Advice and Consent of the Senate, shall appoint Ambassadors, other public Ministers and Consuls, Judges of the supreme Court, and all other Officers of the United States, whose Appointments are not herein otherwise provided for, and which shall be established by Law: but the Congress may by Law vest the Appointment of such inferior Officers, as they think proper, in the President alone, in the Courts of Law, or in the Heads of Departments.

The President shall have Power to fill up all Vacancies that may happen during the Recess of the Senate, by granting Commissions which shall expire at the End of their next Session.

Section. 3.

He shall from time to time give to the Congress Information of the State of the Union, and recommend to their Consideration such Measures as he shall judge necessary and expedient; he may, on extraordinary Occasions, convene both Houses, or either of them, and in Case of Disagreement between them, with Respect to the Time of Adjournment, he may adjourn them to such Time as he shall think proper; he shall receive Ambassadors and other public Ministers; he shall take Care that the Laws be faithfully executed, and shall Commission all the Officers of the United States.

Section. 4.

The President, Vice President and all civil Officers of the United States, shall be removed from Office on Impeachment for, and Conviction of, Treason, Bribery, or other high Crimes and Misdemeanors.

Article. III.

Section. 1.

The judicial Power of the United States, shall be vested in one supreme Court, and in such inferior Courts as the Congress may from time to time ordain and establish. The Judges, both of the supreme and inferior Courts, shall hold their Offices during good Behaviour, and shall, at stated Times, receive for their Services, a Compensation, which shall not be diminished during their Continuance in Office.

Section. 2.

The judicial Power shall extend to all Cases, in Law and Equity, arising under this Constitution, the Laws of the United States, and Treaties made, or which shall be made, under their Authority;—to all Cases affecting Ambassadors, other public Ministers and Consuls;—to all Cases of admiralty and maritime Jurisdiction;—to Controversies to which the United States shall be a Party;—to Controversies between two or more States;— between a State and Citizens of another State,—between Citizens of different States,—between Citizens of the same State claiming Lands under Grants of different States, and between a State, or the Citizens thereof, and foreign States, Citizens or Subjects.

In all Cases affecting Ambassadors, other public Ministers and Consuls, and those in which a State shall be Party, the supreme Court shall have original Jurisdiction. In all the other Cases before mentioned, the supreme Court shall have appellate Jurisdiction, both as to Law and Fact, with such Exceptions, and under such Regulations as the Congress shall make.

The Trial of all Crimes, except in Cases of Impeachment, shall be by Jury; and such Trial shall be held in the State where the said Crimes shall have been committed; but when not committed within any State, the Trial shall be at such Place or Places as the Congress may by Law have directed.

Section. 3.

Treason against the United States, shall consist only in levying War against them, or in adhering to their Enemies, giving them Aid and Comfort. No Person shall be convicted of Treason unless on the Testimony of two Witnesses to the same overt Act, or on Confession in open Court.

The Congress shall have Power to declare the Punishment of Treason, but no Attainder of Treason shall work Corruption of Blood, or Forfeiture except during the Life of the Person attainted.

Article. IV.

Section. 1.

Full Faith and Credit shall be given in each State to the public Acts, Records, and judicial Proceedings of every other State. And the Congress may by general Laws prescribe the Manner in which such Acts, Records and Proceedings shall be proved, and the Effect thereof.

Section. 2.

The Citizens of each State shall be entitled to all Privileges and Immunities of Citizens in the several States.

A Person charged in any State with Treason, Felony, or other Crime, who shall flee from Justice, and be found in another State, shall on Demand of the executive Authority of the State from which he fled, be delivered up, to be removed to the State having Jurisdiction of the Crime.

No Person held to Service or Labour in one State, under the Laws thereof, escaping into another, shall, in Consequence of any Law or Regulation therein, be discharged from such Service or Labour, but shall be delivered up on Claim of the Party to whom such Service or Labour may be due.

Section. 3.

New States may be admitted by the Congress into this Union; but no new State shall be formed or erected within the Jurisdiction of any other State; nor any State be formed by the Junction of two or more States, or Parts of States, without the Consent of the Legislatures of the States concerned as well as of the Congress.

The Congress shall have Power to dispose of and make all needful Rules and Regulations respecting the Territory or other Property belonging to the United States; and nothing in this Constitution shall be so construed as to Prejudice any Claims of the United States, or of any particular State.

Section. 4.

The United States shall guarantee to every State in this Union a Republican Form of Government, and shall protect each of them against Invasion; and on Application of the Legislature, or of the Executive (when the Legislature cannot be convened) against domestic Violence.

Article. V.

The Congress, whenever two thirds of both Houses shall deem it necessary, shall propose Amendments to this Constitution, or, on the Application of the Legislatures of two thirds of the several States, shall call a Convention for proposing Amendments, which, in either Case, shall be valid to all Intents and Purposes, as Part of this Constitution, when ratified by the Legislatures of three fourths of the several States, or by Conventions in three fourths thereof, as the one or the other Mode of Ratification may be proposed by the Congress; Provided that no Amendment which may be made prior to the Year One thousand eight hundred and eight shall in any Manner affect the first and fourth Clauses in the Ninth Section of the first Article; and that no State, without its Consent, shall be deprived of its equal Suffrage in the Senate.

Article. VI.

All Debts contracted and Engagements entered into, before the Adoption of this Constitution, shall be as valid against the United States under this Constitution, as under the Confederation.

This Constitution, and the Laws of the United States which shall be made in Pursuance thereof; and all Treaties made, or which shall be made, under the Authority of the United States, shall be the supreme Law of the Land; and the Judges in every State shall be bound thereby, any Thing in the Constitution or Laws of any State to the Contrary notwithstanding.

The Senators and Representatives before mentioned, and the Members of the several State Legislatures, and all executive and judicial Officers, both of the United States and of the several States, shall be bound by Oath or Affirmation, to support this Constitution; but no religious Test shall ever be required as a Qualification to any Office or public Trust under the United States.

Article. VII.

The Ratification of the Conventions of nine States, shall be sufficient for the Establishment of this Constitution between the States so ratifying the Same.

The Word, "the," being interlined between the seventh and eighth Lines of the first Page, The Word "Thirty" being partly written on an Erazure in the fifteenth Line of the first Page, The Words "is tried" being interlined between the thirty second and thirty third Lines of the first Page and the Word "the" being interlined between the forty third and forty fourth Lines of the second Page.

Attest William Jackson Secretary

done in Convention by the Unanimous Consent of the States present the Seventeenth Day of September in the Year of our Lord one thousand seven hundred and Eighty seven and of the Independance of the United States of America the Twelfth In witness whereof We have hereunto subscribed our Names,

G°. Washington
President and deputy from Virginia

Bill of Rights

Amendment I.

Freedoms, Petitions, Assembly:

Congress shall make no law respecting an establishment of religion, or prohibiting the free exercise thereof; or abridging the freedom of speech, or of the press, or the right of the people peaceably to assemble, and to petition the Government for a redress of grievances.

Amendment II.

Right To Bear Arms:

A well regulated Militia, being necessary to the security of a free State, the right of the people to keep and bear Arms, shall not be infringed.

Amendment III.

Quartering Of Soldiers:

No Soldier shall, in time of peace be quartered in any house, without the consent of the Owner, nor in time of war, but in a manner to be prescribed by law.

Amendment IV.

Search And Arrest:

The right of the people to be secure in their persons, houses, papers, and effects, against unreasonable searches and seizures, shall not be violated, and no Warrants shall issue, but upon probable cause, supported by Oath or affirmation, and particularly describing the place to be searched, and the persons or things to be seized.

Amendment V.

Rights In Criminal Cases:

No person shall be held to answer for a capital, or otherwise infamous crime, unless on a presentment or indictment of a Grand Jury, except in cases arising in the land or naval forces, or in the Militia, when in actual service in time of War or public danger; nor shall any person be subject for the same offence to be twice put in jeopardy of life or limb, nor shall be compelled in any criminal case to be a witness against himself, nor be deprived of life, liberty, or property, without due process of law; nor shall private property be taken for public use, without just compensation.

Amendment VI.

Right To A Fair Trial:

In all criminal prosecutions, the accused shall enjoy the right to a speedy and public trial, by an impartial jury of the State and district wherein the crime shall have been committed; which district shall have been previously ascertained by law, and to be informed of the nature and cause of the accusation; to be confronted with the witnesses against him; to have compulsory process for obtaining witnesses in his favor, and to have the assistance of counsel for his defense.

Amendment VII.

Rights In Civil Cases:

In Suits at common law, where the value in controversy shall exceed twenty dollars, the right of trial by jury shall be preserved, and no fact tried by a jury shall be otherwise re-examined in any Court of the United States, than according to the rules of the common law.

Amendment VIII.

Bail, Fines, Punishment:

Excessive bail shall not be required, nor excessive fines imposed, nor cruel and unusual punishments inflicted.

Amendment IX.

Rights Retained By The People:

The enumeration in the Constitution of certain rights shall not be construed to deny or disparage others retained by the people.

Amendment X.

States' Rights:

The powers not delegated to the United States by the Constitution, nor prohibited by it to the States, are reserved to the States respectively, or to the people.

Amendment XI.

Lawsuits Against States:

The Judicial power of the United States shall not be construed to extend to any suit in law or equity, commenced or prosecuted against one of the United States by Citizens of another State, or by Citizens or Subjects of any Foreign State.

February 7, 1795.

Amendment XII.

Presidential Elections:

The Electors shall meet in their respective states, and vote by ballot for President and Vice-President, one of whom, at least, shall not be an inhabitant of the same state with themselves; they shall name in their ballots the person voted for as President, and in distinct ballots the person voted for as Vice-President, and they shall make distinct lists of all persons voted for as President, and of all persons voted for as Vice-President, and of the number of votes for each, which lists they shall sign and certify, and transmit sealed to the seat of the government of the United States, directed to the President of the Senate;--The President of the Senate shall, in the presence of the Senate and House of Representatives, open all the certificates and the votes shall then be counted;--The person having the greatest number of votes for President, shall be the President, if such number be a majority of the whole number of Electors appointed; and if no person have such majority, then from the persons having the highest numbers not exceeding three on the list of those voted for as President, the House of Representatives shall chuse immediately, by ballot, the President. But in choosing the President, the votes shall be taken by states, the representation from each state having one vote; a quorum for this purpose shall consist of a member or members from two-thirds of the states, and a majority of all the states shall be necessary to a choice. [And if the House of Representatives shall not chuse a President whenever the right of choice shall devolve upon them, before the fourth day of March next following, then the Vice-President shall act as President, as in the case of the death or other constitutional disability of the President.]* The person having the greatest number of votes as Vice-President, shall be the Vice-President, if such number be a majority of the whole number of Electors appointed, and if no person have a majority, then from the two highest numbers on the list, the Senate shall chuse the Vice-President; a quorum for the purpose shall consist of two-thirds of the whole number of Senators, and a majority of the whole number shall be necessary to a choice. But no person constitutionally ineligible to the office of President shall be eligible to that of Vice-President of the United States.

June 15, 1804.
Superseded by Section 3 of the Twentieth Amendment.

Amendment XIII.

Abolition Of Slavery:

Section 1. Neither slavery nor involuntary servitude, except as a punishment for crime whereof the party shall have been duly convicted, shall exist within the United States, or any place subject to their jurisdiction.

Section 2. Congress shall have power to enforce these article by appropriate legislation.

December 6, 1865.

Amendment XIV.

Civil Rights:

Section 1. All persons born or naturalized in the United States and subject to the jurisdiction thereof, are citizens of the United States and of the State wherein they reside. No State shall make or enforce any law which shall abridge the privileges or immunities of citizens of the United States; nor shall any State deprive any person of life, liberty, or property, without due process of law; nor deny to any person within its jurisdiction the equal protection of the laws.

Section 2. Representatives shall be apportioned among the several States according to their respective numbers, counting the whole number of persons in each State, excluding Indians not taxed. But when the right to vote at any election for the choice of electors for President and Vice President of the United States, Representatives in Congress, the Executive and Judicial officers of a State, or the members of the Legislature thereof, is denied to any of the male inhabitants of such State, being twenty-one years of age, and citizens of the United States, or in any way abridged, except for participation in rebellion, or other crime, the basis of representation therein shall be reduced in the proportion which the number of such male citizens shall bear to the whole number of male citizens twenty-one years of age in such State.

Section 3. No person shall be a Senator or Representative in Congress, or elector of President and Vice President, or hold any office, civil or military, under the United States, or under any State, who, having previously taken an oath, as a member of Congress, or as an officer of the United States, or as a member of any State legislature, or as an executive or judicial officer of any State, to support the Constitution of the United States, shall have engaged in insurrection or rebellion against the same, or given aid or comfort to the enemies thereof. But Congress may by a vote of two-thirds of each House, remove such disability.

Section 4. The validity of the public debt of the United States, authorized by law, including debts incurred for payment of pensions and bounties for services in suppressing insurrection or rebellion, shall not be questioned. But neither the United States nor any State shall assume or pay any debt or obligation incurred in aid of insurrection or rebellion against the United States, or any claim for the loss or emancipation of any slave; but all such debts, obligations and claims shall be held illegal and void.

Section 5. The Congress shall have power to enforce, by appropriate legislation, the provisions of this article.

July 9, 1868.

Amendment XV.

Black Suffrage:

Section 1. The right of citizens of the United States to vote shall not be denied or abridged by the United States or by any State on account of race, color, or previous condition of servitude.

Section 2. The Congress shall have power to enforce this article by appropriate legislation.

February 3, 1870.

Amendment XVI.

Income Taxes:

The Congress shall have power to lay and collect taxes on incomes, from whatever source derived, without apportionment among the several States, and without regard to any census or enumeration.

February 3, 1913.

Amendment XVII.

Senatorial Elections:

The Senate of the United States shall be composed of two senators from each State, elected by the people thereof, for six years; and each Senator shall have one vote. The electors in each State shall have the qualifications requisite for electors of the most numerous branch of the State legislature.

When vacancies happen in the representation of any State in the Senate, the executive authority of such State shall issue writs of election to fill such vacancies: *Provided*, That the legislature of any State may empower the executive thereof to make temporary appointments until the people fill the vacancies by election as the legislature may direct.

This amendment shall not be so construed as to affect the election or term of any Senator chosen before it becomes valid as part of the Constitution.

April 8, 1913.

Amendment XVIII.

Prohibition Of Liquor:

Section 1. After one year from the ratification of this article, the manufacture, sale, or transportation of intoxicating liquors within, the importation thereof into, or the exportation thereof from the United States and all territory subject to the jurisdiction thereof for beverage purposes is hereby prohibited.

Section 2. The Congress and the several States shall have concurrent power to enforce this article by appropriate legislation.

Section 3. This article shall be inoperative unless it shall have been ratified as an amendment to the Constitution by the legislatures of the several States, as provided in the Constitution, within seven years from the date of the submission hereof to the States by the Congress.

January 16, 1919. Repealed by the Twenty-First, December 5, 1933.

Amendment XIX.

Women's Suffrage:

The right of citizens of the United States to vote shall not be denied or abridged by the United States or by any States on account of sex.

Congress shall have power to enforce this article by appropriate legislation.

August 18, 1920.

Amendment XX.

Terms Of Office:

Section 1. The terms of the President and Vice President shall end at noon the 20th day of January, and the terms of Senators and Representatives at noon on the 3d day of January, of the years in which such terms would have ended if this article had not been ratified; and the terms of their successors shall then begin.

Section 2. The Congress shall assemble at least once in every year, and such meeting shall begin at noon on the 3d day of January, unless they shall by law appoint a different day.

Section 3. If, at the time fixed for the beginning of the term of the President, the President elect shall have died, the Vice President elect shall become President. If a President shall not have been chosen before the time fixed for the beginning of his term, or if the President elect shall have failed to qualify, then the Vice President elect shall act as President until a President shall have qualified; and the Congress may by law provide for the case wherein neither a President elect nor a Vice President elect shall have qualified, declaring who shall then act as President, or the manner in which one who is to act shall be selected, and such person shall act accordingly until a President or Vice President shall have qualified.

Section 4. The Congress may by law provide for the case of the death of any of the persons from whom the House of Representatives may chuse a President whenever the right of choice shall have devolved upon them, and for the case of the death of any of the persons from whom the Senate may chuse a Vice President whenever the right of choice shall have devolved upon them.

Section 5. Sections 1 and 2 shall take effect on the 15th day of October following the ratification of this article.

Section 6. This article shall be inoperative unless it shall have been ratified as an amendment to the Constitution by the legislatures of three-fourths of the several States within seven years from the date of its submission.

January 23, 1933.

Amendment XXI.

Repeal Of Prohibition:

Section 1. The eighteenth article of amendment to the Constitution of the United States is hereby repealed.

Section 2. The transportation or importation into any State, Territory, or possession of the United States for delivery or use therein of intoxicating liquors, in violation of the laws thereof, is hereby prohibited.

Section 3. The article shall be inoperative unless it shall have been ratified as an amendment to the Constitution by conventions in the several States, as provided in the Constitution, within seven years from the date of the submission hereof to the States by the Congress.

December 5, 1933.

Amendment XXII.

Term Limits For The Presidency:

Section 1. No person shall be elected to the office of the President more than twice, and no person who has held the office of President, or acted as President, for more than two years of a term to which some other person was elected President shall be elected to the office of the President more than once. But this Article shall not apply to any person holding the office of President when this Article was proposed by the Congress, and shall not prevent any person who may be holding the office of President, or acting as President, during the term within which this Article becomes operative from holding the office of President or acting as President during the remainder of such term.

Section 2. This article shall be inoperative unless it shall have been ratified as an amendment to the Constitution by the legislatures of three-fourths of the several States within seven years from the date of its submission to the States by the Congress.

February 27, 1951.

Amendment XXIII.

Washington, D.C., Suffrage:

Section 1. The District constituting the seat of government of the United States shall appoint in such manner as the Congress may direct:

A number of electors of President and Vice President equal to the whole number of Senators and Representatives in Congress to which the District would be entitled if it were a state, but in no event more than the least populous State; they shall be in addition to those appointed by the States, but they shall be considered, for the purposes of the election of President and Vice President, to be electors appointed by a State; and they shall meet in the District and perform such duties as provided by the twelfth article of amendment.

Section 2. The Congress shall have power to enforce this article by appropriate legislation.

March 29, 1961.

Amendment XXIV.

Abolition Of Poll Taxes:

Section 1. The right of citizens of the United States to vote in any primary or other election for President or Vice President, for electors for President or Vice President, or for Senator or Representative in Congress, shall not be denied or abridged by the United States or any State by reason of failure to pay any poll tax or other tax.

Section 2. The Congress shall have power to enforce this article by appropriate legislation.

January 23, 1964.

Amendment XXV.

Presidential Succession:

Section 1. In case of the removal of the President from office or of his death or resignation, the Vice President shall become President.

Section 2. Whenever there is a vacancy in the office of the Vice President, the President shall nominate a Vice President who shall take office upon confirmation by a majority vote of both Houses of Congress.

Section 3. Whenever the President transmits to the President pro tempore of the Senate and the Speaker of the House of Representatives his written declaration that he is unable to discharge the powers and duties of his office, and until he transmits to them a written declaration to the contrary, such powers and duties shall be discharged by the Vice President as Acting President.

Section 4. Whenever the Vice President and a majority of either the principal officers of the executive departments or of such other body as Congress may by law provide, transmit to the President pro tempore of the Senate and the Speaker of the House of Representatives their written declaration that the President is unable to discharge the powers and duties of his office, the Vice President shall immediately assume the powers and duties of the office as Acting President.

Thereafter, when the President transmits to the President pro tempore of the Senate and the Speaker of the House of Representatives his written declaration that no inability exists, he shall resume the powers and duties of his office unless the Vice President and a majority of either the principal officers of the executive department or of such other body as Congress may by law provide, transmit within four days to the President pro tempore of the Senate and the Speaker of the House of Representatives their written declaration that the President is unable to discharge the powers and duties of his office. Thereupon Congress shall decide the issue, assembling within forty-eight hours for that purpose if not in session. If the Congress, within twenty-one days after receipt of the latter written declaration, or, if Congress is not in session, within twenty-one days after Congress is required to assemble, determines by two-thirds vote of both Houses that the President is unable to discharge the powers and duties of his office, the Vice President shall continue to discharge the same as Acting President; otherwise, the President shall resume the powers and duties of his office.

February 10, 1967.

Amendment XXVI.

18-Year-Old Suffrage:

Section 1. The right of citizens of the United States, who are eighteen years of age or older, to vote shall not be denied or abridged by the United States or by any State on account of age.

Section 2. The Congress shall have power to enforce this article by appropriate legislation.

June 30, 1971.

Amendment XXVII.

Congressional Pay Raises:

No law, varying the compensation for the services of the Senators and Representatives, shall take effect, until an election of Representatives shall have intervened.

Addenda Part II.: Notable Speeches

George Washington's Farewell Address

FRIENDS AND FELLOW-CITIZENS:

The period for a new election of a citizen, to administer the executive government of the United States, being not far distant, and the time actually arrived, when your thoughts must be employed designating the person, who is to be clothed with that important trust, it appears to me proper, especially as it may conduce to a more distinct expression of the public voice, that I should now apprize you of the resolution I have formed, to decline being considered among the number of those out of whom a choice is to be made.

I beg you at the same time to do me the justice to be assured that this resolution has not been taken without a strict regard to all the considerations appertaining to the relation which binds a dutiful citizen to his country; and that in withdrawing the tender of service, which silence in my situation might imply, I am influenced by no diminution of zeal for your future interest, no deficiency of grateful respect for your past kindness, but am supported by a full conviction that the step is compatible with both.

The acceptance of, and continuance hitherto in, the office to which your suffrages have twice called me, have been a uniform sacrifice of inclination to the opinion of duty, and to a deference for what appeared to be your desire. I constantly hoped that it would have been much earlier in my power, consistent with motivations which I was not at liberty to disregard, to return to that retirement from which I had been reluctantly drawn. The strength of my inclination to do this, previous to the last election, had even led to the preparation of an address to declare it to you; but mature reflection on the then perplexed and critical posture of our affairs with foreign nations, and the unanimous advice of persons entitled to my confidence impelled me to abandon the idea.

I rejoice, that the state of your concerns, external as well as internal, no longer renders the pursuit of inclination incompatible with the sentiment of duty, or propriety; and am persuaded, whatever partiality may be retained for my services, that, in the present circumstances of our country, you will not disapprove my determination to retire.

The impressions, with which I first undertook the arduous trust, were explained on the proper occasion. In the discharge of this trust, I will only say, that I have, with good intentions, contributed towards the organization and administration of the government the best exertions of which a very fallible judgment was capable. Not unconscious, in the outset, of the inferiority of my qualifications, experience in my own eyes, perhaps still more in the eyes of others, has strengthened the motives to diffidence of myself; and every day the increasing weight of years admonishes me more and more, that the shade of retirement is as necessary to me as it will be welcome. Satisfied, that, if any circumstances have given peculiar value to my services, they were temporary, I have the consolation to believe, that, while choice and prudence invite me to quit the political scene, patriotism does not forbid it.

In looking forward to the moment, which is intended to terminate the career of my public life, my feelings do not permit me to suspend the deep acknowledgment of that debt of gratitude, which I owe to my beloved country for the many honors it has conferred upon me; still more for the steadfast confidence with which it has supported me; and for the opportunities I have thence enjoyed of manifesting my inviolable attachment, by services faithful and persevering, though in usefulness unequal to my zeal. If benefits have resulted to our country from these services, let it always be remembered to your praise, and as an instructive example in our annals, that under circumstances in which the passions, agitated in every direction, were liable to mislead, amidst appearances sometimes dubious, vicissitudes of fortune often discouraging, in situations in which not unfrequently want of success has countenanced the spirit of criticism, the constancy of your support was the essential prop of the efforts, and a guarantee of the plans by which they were effected.

Profoundly penetrated with this idea, I shall carry it with me to my grave, as a strong incitement to unceasing vows that Heaven may continue to you the choicest tokens of its beneficence; that your union and brotherly affection may be perpetual; that the free constitution, which is the work of your hands, may be sacredly maintained; that its administration in every department may be stamped with wisdom and virtue; that, in *fine*, the happiness of the people of these States, under the auspices of liberty, may be made complete, by so careful a preservation and so prudent a use of this blessing, as will acquire to them the glory of recommending it to the applause, the affection, and adoption of every nation, which is yet a stranger to it.

Here, perhaps I ought to stop. But a solicitude for your welfare which cannot end but with my life, and the apprehension of danger, natural to that solicitude, urge me, on an occasion like the present, to offer to your solemn contemplation, and to recommend to your frequent review, some sentiments which are the result of much reflection, of no inconsiderable observation, and which appear to me all-important to the permanency of your felicity as a people. These will be offered to you with the more freedom, as you can only see in them the disinterested warnings of a parting friend, who can possibly have no personal motive to bias his counsel. Nor can I forget, as an encouragement to it, your indulgent reception of my sentiments on a former and not dissimilar occasion.

Interwoven as is the love of liberty with every ligament of your hearts, no recommendation of mine is necessary to fortify or confirm the attachment.

The unity of Government, which constitutes you one people, is also now dear to you. It is justly so; for it is a main pillar in the edifice of your real independence, the support of your tranquility at home, your peace abroad; of your safety; of your prosperity; of that very Liberty, which you so highly prize. But as it is easy to foresee, that, from different causes and from different quarters, much pains will be taken, many artifices employed, to weaken in your minds the conviction of this truth; as this is the point in your political fortress against which the batteries of internal and external enemies will be most constantly and actively, though often covertly and insidiously, directed, it is of infinite moment, that you should properly estimate the immense value of your national Union to your collective and individual happiness; that you should cherish a cordial, habitual, and immovable attachment to it; accustoming yourselves to think and speak of it as of the Palladium of your political safety and prosperity; watching for its preservation with jealous anxiety; discountenancing whatever may suggest even a suspicion, that it can in any event be abandoned; and indignantly frowning upon the first dawning of every attempt to alienate any portion of our country from the rest, or to enfeeble the sacred ties which now link together the various parts.

For this you have every inducement of sympathy and interest. Citizens, by birth or choice, of a common country, that country has a right to concentrate your affections. The name of American, which belongs to you, in your national capacity, must always exalt the just pride of Patriotism, more than any appellation derived from local discriminations.

With slight shades of difference, you have the same religion, manners, habits, and political principles. You have in a common cause fought and triumphed together; the Independence and Liberty you possess are the work of joint counsels, and joint efforts, of common dangers, sufferings, and successes.

But these considerations, however powerfully they address themselves to your sensibility, are greatly outweighed by those, which apply more immediately to your interest. Here every portion of our country finds the most commanding motives for carefully guarding and preserving the Union of the whole.

The North, in an unrestrained intercourse with the South, protected by the equal laws of a common government, finds, in the productions of the latter, great additional resources of maritime and commercial enterprise and precious materials of manufacturing industry. The South, in the same intercourse, benefiting by the agency of the North, sees its agriculture grow and its commerce expand. Turning partly into its own channels the seamen of the North, it finds its particular navigation invigorated; and, while it contributes, in different ways, to nourish and increase the general mass of the national navigation, it looks forward to the protection of a maritime strength, to which itself is unequally adapted. The East, in a like intercourse with the West, already finds, and in the progressive improvement of interior communications by land and water, will more and more find, a valuable vent for the commodities which it brings from abroad, or manufactures at home. The West derives from the East supplies requisite to its growth and comfort, and, what is perhaps of still greater consequence, it must of necessity owe the secure enjoyment of indispensable outlets for its own productions to the weight, influence, and the future maritime strength of the Atlantic side of the Union, directed by an indissoluble community of interest as one nation. Any other tenure by which the West can hold this essential advantage, whether derived from its own separate strength, or from an apostate and unnatural connexion with any foreign power, must be intrinsically precarious.

While, then, every part of our country thus feels an immediate and particular interest in Union, all the parts combined cannot fail to find in the united mass of means and efforts, greater strength, greater resource, proportionably greater security from external danger, a less frequent interruption of their peace by foreign nations; and, what is of inestimable value, they must derive from Union an exemption from those broils and wars between themselves, which so frequently afflict neighbouring countries not tied together by the same governments, which their own rivalships alone would be sufficient to produce, but which opposite foreign alliances, attachments, and intrigues would stimulate and embitter. Hence, likewise, they will avoid the necessity of those overgrown military establishments, which, under any form of government, are inauspicious to liberty, and which are to be regarded as particularly hostile to Republican Liberty. In this sense it is, that your Union ought to be considered as a main prop of your liberty, and that the love of the one ought to endear to you the preservation of the other.

These considerations speak a persuasive language to every reflecting and virtuous mind, and exhibit the continuance of the union as a primary object of Patriotic desire. Is there a doubt, whether a common government can embrace so large a sphere? Let experience solve it. To listen to mere speculation in such a case is criminal. We are authorized to hope, that a proper organization of the whole, with the auxiliary agency of governments for the respective subdivisions, will afford a happy issue to the experiment. It is well worth a fair and full experiment. With such powerful and obvious motives to Union, affecting all parts of our country, while experience shall not have demonstrated its impracticability, there will always be reason to distrust the patriotism of those, who in any quarter may endeavour to weaken its bands.

In contemplating the causes, which may disturb our Union, it occurs as matter of serious concern, that any ground should have been furnished for characterizing parties by Geographical discriminations, Northern and Southern, Atlantic and Western; whence designing men may endeavour to excite a belief, that there is a real difference of local interests and views. One of the expedients of party to acquire influence, within particular districts, is to misrepresent the opinions and aims of other districts. You cannot shield yourselves too much against the jealousies and heart-burnings, which spring from these misrepresentations; they tend to render alien to each other those, who ought to be bound together by fraternal affection. The inhabitants of our western country have lately had a useful lesson on this head; they have seen, in the negotiation by the Executive, and in the unanimous ratification by the Senate, of the treaty with Spain, and in the universal satisfaction at that event, throughout the United States, a decisive proof of how unfounded were the suspicions propagated among them of a policy in the General Government and in the Atlantic States unfriendly to their interests in regard to the Mississippi; they have been witnesses to the formation of two treaties, that with Great Britain, and that with Spain, which secure to them every thing they could desire, in respect to our foreign relations, towards confirming their prosperity. Will it not be their wisdom to rely for the preservation of these advantages on the union by which they were procured? Will they not henceforth be deaf to those advisers, if such there are, who would sever them from their brethren, and connect them with aliens?

To the efficacy and permanency of your Union, a Government for the whole is indispensable. No alliances, however strict between the parts, can be an adequate substitute; they must inevitably experience the infractions and interruptions which all alliances in all times have experienced. Sensible of this momentous truth, you have improved upon your first essay, by the adoption of a Constitution of Government better calculated than your former for an intimate Union, and for the efficacious management of your common concerns.

This Government, the offspring of our own choice, uninfluenced and unawed, adopted upon full investigation and mature deliberation, completely free in its principles, in the distribution of its powers, uniting security with energy, and containing within itself a provision for its own amendment, has a just claim to your confidence and your support. Respect for its authority, compliance with its laws, acquiescence in its measures, are duties enjoined by the fundamental maxims of true Liberty. The basis of our political systems is the right of the people to make and to alter their Constitutions of Government. But the Constitution which at any time exists, until changed by an explicit and authentic act of the whole people, is sacredly obligatory upon all. The very idea of the power and the right of the people to establish Government presupposes the duty of every individual to obey the established Government.

All obstructions to the execution of the Laws, all combinations and associations, under whatever plausible character, with the real design to direct, control, counteract, or awe the regular deliberation and action of the constituted authorities, are destructive of this fundamental principle, and of fatal tendency. They serve to organize faction, to give it an artificial and extraordinary force; to put, in the place of the delegated will of the nation, the will of a party, often a small but artful and enterprising minority of the community; and, according to the alternate triumphs of different parties, to make the public administration the mirror of the ill-concerted and incongruous projects of faction, rather than the organ of consistent and wholesome plans digested by common counsels, and modified by mutual interests.

However combinations or associations of the above description may now and then answer popular ends, they are likely, in the course of time and things, to become potent engines, by which cunning, ambitious, and unprincipled men will be enabled to subvert the power of the people, and to usurp for themselves the reins of government; destroying afterwards the very engines, which have lifted them to unjust dominion.

Towards the preservation of your government, and the permanency of your present happy state, it is requisite, not only that you steadily discountenance irregular oppositions to its acknowledged authority, but also that you resist with care the spirit of innovation upon its principles, however specious the pretexts. One method of assault may be to effect, in the forms of the constitution, alterations, which will impair the energy of the system, and thus to undermine what cannot be directly overthrown. In all the changes to which you may be invited, remember that time and habit are at least as necessary to fix the true character of governments, as of other human institutions; that experience is the surest standard, by which to test the real tendency of the existing constitution of a country; that facility in changes, upon the credit of mere hypothesis and opinion, exposes to perpetual change, from the endless variety of hypothesis and opinion; and remember, especially, that, for the efficient management of our common interests, in a country so extensive as ours, a government of as much vigor as is consistent with the perfect security of liberty is indispensable.

Liberty itself will find in such a government, with powers properly distributed and adjusted, its surest guardian. It is, indeed, little else than a name, where the government is too feeble to withstand the enterprises of faction, to confine each member of the society within the limits prescribed by the laws, and to maintain all in the secure and tranquil enjoyment of the rights of person and property.

I have already intimated to you the danger of parties in the state, with particular reference to the founding of them on geographical discriminations. Let me now take a more comprehensive view, and warn you in the most solemn manner against the baneful effects of the spirit of party, generally.

This spirit, unfortunately, is inseparable from our nature, having its root in the strongest passions of the human mind. It exists under different shapes in all governments, more or less stifled, controlled, or repressed; but, in those of the popular form, it is seen in its greatest rankness, and is truly their worst enemy.

The alternate domination of one faction over another, sharpened by the spirit of revenge, natural to party dissension, which in different ages and countries has perpetrated the most horrid enormities, is itself a frightful despotism. But this leads at length to a more formal and permanent despotism. The disorders and miseries, which result, gradually incline the minds of men to seek security and repose in the absolute power of an individual; and sooner or later the chief of some prevailing faction, more able or more fortunate than his competitors, turns this disposition to the purposes of his own elevation, on the ruins of Public Liberty.

Without looking forward to an extremity of this kind, which nevertheless ought not to be entirely out of sight, the common and continual mischiefs of the spirit of party are sufficient to make it the interest and duty of a wise people to discourage and restrain it.

It serves always to distract the Public Councils, and enfeeble the Public Administration. It agitates the Community with ill-founded jealousies and false alarms; kindles the animosity of one part against another, foments occasionally riot and insurrection. It opens the door to foreign influence and corruption, which find a facilitated access to the government itself through the channels of party passions. Thus the policy and the will of one country are subjected to the policy and will of another. There is an opinion, that parties in free countries are useful checks upon the administration of the Government, and serve to keep alive the spirit of Liberty. This within certain limits is probably true; and in Governments of a Monarchical cast, Patriotism may look with indulgence, if not with favor, upon the spirit of party. But in those of the popular character, in Governments purely elective, it is a spirit not to be encouraged. From their natural tendency, it is certain there will always be enough of that spirit for every salutary purpose. And, there being constant danger of excess, the effort ought to be, by force of public opinion, to mitigate and assuage it. A fire not to be quenched, it demands a uniform vigilance to prevent its bursting into a flame, lest, instead of warming, it should consume.

It is important, likewise, that the habits of thinking in a free country should inspire caution, in those intrusted with its administration, to confine themselves within their respective constitutional spheres, avoiding in the exercise of the powers of one department to encroach upon another. The spirit of encroachment tends to consolidate the powers of all the departments in one, and thus to create, whatever the form of government, a real despotism. A just estimate of that love of power, and proneness to abuse it, which predominates in the human heart, is sufficient to satisfy us of the truth of this position. The necessity of reciprocal checks in the exercise of political power, by dividing and distributing it into different depositories, and constituting each the Guardian of the Public Weal against invasions by the others, has been evinced by experiments ancient and modern; some of them in our country and under our own eyes. To preserve them must be as necessary as to institute them. If, in the opinion of the people, the distribution or modification of the constitutional powers be in any particular wrong, let it be corrected by an amendment in the way, which the constitution designates. But let there be no change by usurpation; for, though this, in one instance, may be the instrument of good, it is the customary weapon by which free governments are destroyed. The precedent must always greatly overbalance in permanent evil any partial or transient benefit, which the use can at any time yield.

Of all the dispositions and habits, which lead to political prosperity, Religion and Morality are indispensable supports. In vain would that man claim the tribute of Patriotism, who should labor to subvert these great pillars of human happiness, these firmest props of the duties of Men and Citizens. The mere Politician, equally with the pious man, ought to respect and to cherish them. A volume could not trace all their connexions with private and public felicity. Let it simply be asked, Where is the security for property, for reputation, for life, if the sense of religious obligation desert the oaths, which are the instruments of investigation in Courts of Justice? And let us with caution indulge the supposition, that morality can be maintained without religion. Whatever may be conceded to the influence of refined education on minds of peculiar structure, reason and experience both forbid us to expect, that national morality can prevail in exclusion of religious principle.

It is substantially true, that virtue or morality is a necessary spring of popular government. The rule, indeed, extends with more or less force to every species of free government. Who, that is a sincere friend to it, can look with indifference upon attempts to shake the foundation of the fabric? Promote, then, as an object of primary importance, institutions for the general diffusion of knowledge. In proportion as the structure of a government gives force to public opinion, it is essential that public opinion should be enlightened.

As a very important source of strength and security, cherish public credit. One method of preserving it is, to use it as sparingly as possible; avoiding occasions of expense by cultivating peace, but remembering also that timely disbursements to prepare for danger frequently prevent much greater disbursements to repel it; avoiding likewise the accumulation of debt, not only by shunning occasions of expense, but by vigorous exertions in time of peace to discharge the debts, which unavoidable wars may have occasioned, not ungenerously throwing upon posterity the burthen, which we ourselves ought to bear. The execution of these maxims belongs to your representatives, but it is necessary that public opinion should cooperate. To facilitate to them the performance of their duty, it is essential that you should practically bear in mind, that towards the payment of debts there must be Revenue; that to have Revenue there must be taxes; that no taxes can be devised, which are not more or less inconvenient and unpleasant; that the intrinsic embarrassment, inseparable from the selection of the proper objects, which is always a choice of difficulties, ought to be a decisive motive for a candid construction of the conduct of the government in making it, and for a spirit of acquiescence in the measures for obtaining revenue, which the public exigencies may at any time dictate.

Observe good faith and justice towards all Nations; cultivate peace and harmony with all. Religion and Morality enjoin this conduct; and can it be, that good policy does not equally enjoin it? It will be worthy of a free, enlightened, and, at no distant period, a great Nation, to give to mankind the magnanimous and too novel example of a people always guided by an exalted justice and benevolence. Who can doubt, that, in the course of time and things, the fruits of such a plan would richly repay any temporary advantages, which might be lost by a steady adherence to it? Can it be, that Providence has not connected the permanent felicity of a Nation with its Virtue? The experiment, at least, is recommended by every sentiment which ennobles human nature.
Alas! Is it rendered impossible by its vices?

In the execution of such a plan, nothing is more essential, than that permanent, inveterate antipathies against particular Nations, and passionate attachments for others, should be excluded; and that, in place of them, just and amicable feelings towards all should be cultivated.

The Nation, which indulges towards another an habitual hatred, or an habitual fondness, is in some degree a slave. It is a slave to its animosity or to its affection, either of which is sufficient to lead it astray from its duty and its interest. Antipathy in one nation against another disposes each more readily to offer insult and injury, to lay hold of slight causes of umbrage, and to be haughty and intractable, when accidental or trifling occasions of dispute occur. Hence frequent collisions, obstinate, envenomed, and bloody contests. The Nation, prompted by ill-will and resentment, sometimes impels to war the Government, contrary to the best calculations of policy. The Government sometimes participates in the national propensity, and adopts through passion what reason would reject; at other times, it makes the animosity of the nation subservient to projects of hostility instigated by pride, ambition, and other sinister and pernicious motives. The peace often, sometimes perhaps the liberty of Nations, has been the victim.

So likewise, a passionate attachment of one Nation for another produces a variety of evils. Sympathy for the favorite Nation, facilitating the illusion of an imaginary common interest, in cases where no real common interest exists, and infusing into one the enmities of the other, betrays the former into a participation in the quarrels and wars of the latter, without adequate inducement or justification. It leads also to concessions to the favorite Nation of privileges denied to others, which is apt doubly to injure the Nation making the concessions; by unnecessarily parting with what ought to have been retained; and by exciting jealousy, ill-will, and a disposition to retaliate, in the parties from whom equal privileges are withheld.

And it gives to ambitious, corrupted, or deluded citizens, (who devote themselves to the favorite nation,) facility to betray or sacrifice the interests of their own country, without odium, sometimes even with popularity; gilding, with the appearances of a virtuous sense of obligation, a commendable deference for public opinion, or a laudable zeal for public good, the base or foolish compliances of ambition, corruption, or infatuation.

As avenues to foreign influence in innumerable ways, such attachments are particularly alarming to the truly enlightened and independent Patriot. How many opportunities do they afford to tamper with domestic factions, to practise the arts of seduction, to mislead public opinion, to influence or awe the Public Councils! Such an attachment of a small or weak, towards a great and powerful nation, dooms the former to be the satellite of the latter.

Against the insidious wiles of foreign influence, I conjure you to believe me, fellow-citizens, the jealousy of a free people ought to be constantly awake; since history and experience prove, that foreign influence is one of the most baneful foes of Republican Government. But that jealousy, to be useful, must be impartial; else it becomes the instrument of the very influence to be avoided, instead of a defence against it. Excessive partiality for one foreign nation, and excessive dislike of another, cause those whom they actuate to see danger only on one side, and serve to veil and even second the arts of influence on the other. Real patriots, who may resist the intrigues of the favorite, are liable to become suspected and odious; while its tools and dupes usurp the applause and confidence of the people, to surrender their interests.

The great rule of conduct for us, in regard to foreign nations, is, in extending our commercial relations, to have with them as little political connexion as possible. So far as we have already formed engagements, let them be fulfilled with perfect good faith. Here let us stop.

Europe has a set of primary interests, which to us have none, or a very remote relation. Hence she must be engaged in frequent controversies, the causes of which are essentially foreign to our concerns. Hence, therefore, it must be unwise in us to implicate ourselves, by artificial ties, in the ordinary vicissitudes of her politics, or the ordinary combinations and collisions of her friendships or enmities. Our detached and distant situation invites and enables us to pursue a different course. If we remain one people, under an efficient government, the period is not far off, when we may defy material injury from external annoyance; when we may take such an attitude as will cause the neutrality, we may at any time resolve upon, to be scrupulously respected; when belligerent nations, under the impossibility of making acquisitions upon us, will not lightly hazard the giving us provocation; when we may chuse peace or war, as our interest, guided by justice, shall counsel.

Why forego the advantages of so peculiar a situation? Why quit our own to stand upon foreign ground? Why, by interweaving our destiny with that of any part of Europe, entangle our peace and prosperity in the toils of European ambition, rivalship, interest, humor, or caprice?

It is our true policy to steer clear of permanent alliances with any portion of the foreign world; so far, I mean, as we are now at liberty to do it; for let me not be understood as capable of patronizing infidelity to existing engagements. I hold the maxim no less applicable to public than to private affairs, that honesty is always the best policy. I repeat it, therefore, let those engagements be observed in their genuine sense. But, in my opinion, it is unnecessary and would be unwise to extend them.

Taking care always to keep ourselves, by suitable establishments, on a respectable defensive posture, we may safely trust to temporary alliances for extraordinary emergencies.

Harmony, liberal intercourse with all nations, are recommended by policy, humanity, and interest. But even our commercial policy should hold an equal and impartial hand; neither seeking nor granting exclusive favors or preferences; consulting the natural course of things; diffusing and diversifying by gentle means the streams of commerce, but forcing nothing; establishing, with powers so disposed, in order to give trade a stable course, to define the rights of our merchants, and to enable the government to support them, conventional rules of intercourse, the best that present circumstances and mutual opinion will permit, but temporary, and liable to be from time to time abandoned or varied, as experience and circumstances shall dictate; constantly keeping in view, that it is folly in one nation to look for disinterested favors from another; that it must pay with a portion of its independence for whatever it may accept under that character; that, by such acceptance, it may place itself in the condition of having given equivalents for nominal favors, and yet of being reproached with ingratitude for not giving more. There can be no greater error than to expect or calculate upon real favors from nation to nation. It is an illusion, which experience must cure, which a just pride ought to discard.

In offering to you, my countrymen, these counsels of an old and affectionate friend, I dare not hope they will make the strong and lasting impression I could wish; that they will control the usual current of the passions, or prevent our nation from running the course, which has hitherto
marked the destiny of nations.

But, if I may even flatter myself, that they may be productive of some partial benefit, some occasional good; that they may now and then recur to moderate the fury of party spirit, to warn against the mischiefs of foreign intrigue, to guard against the impostures of pretended patriotism; this hope will be a full recompense for the solicitude for your welfare, by which they have been dictated.

How far in the discharge of my official duties, I have been guided by the principles which have been delineated, the public records and other evidences of my conduct must witness to you and to the world. To myself, the assurance of my own conscience is, that I have at least believed myself to be guided by them.

In relation to the still subsisting war in Europe, my Proclamation of the 22d of April 1793, is the index to my Plan. Sanctioned by your approving voice, and by that of your Representatives in both Houses of Congress, the spirit of that measure has continually governed me, uninfluenced by any attempts to deter or divert me from it.

After deliberate examination, with the aid of the best lights I could obtain, I was well satisfied that our country, under all the circumstances of the case, had a right to take, and was bound in duty and interest to take, a neutral position. Having taken it, I determined, as far as should depend upon me, to maintain it, with moderation, perseverance, and firmness.

The considerations, which respect the right to hold this conduct, it is not necessary on this occasion to detail. I will only observe, that, according to my understanding of the matter, that right, so far from being denied by any of the Belligerent Powers, has been virtually admitted by all.

The duty of holding a neutral conduct may be inferred, without any thing more, from the obligation which justice and humanity impose on every nation, in cases in which it is free to act, to maintain inviolate the relations of peace and amity towards other nations.

The inducements of interest for observing that conduct will best be referred to your own reflections and experience. With me, a predominant motive has been to endeavour to gain time to our country to settle and mature its yet recent institutions, and to progress without interruption to that degree of strength and consistency, which is necessary to give it, humanly speaking, the command of its own fortunes. Though, in reviewing the incidents of my administration, I am unconscious of intentional error, I am nevertheless too sensible of my defects not to think it probable that I may have committed many errors. Whatever they may be, I fervently beseech the Almighty to avert or mitigate the evils to which they may tend. I shall also carry with me the hope, that my Country will never cease to view them with indulgence; and that, after forty-five years of my life dedicated to its service with an upright zeal,
the faults of incompetent abilities will be consigned to oblivion, as myself must soon be
to the mansions of rest.

Relying on its kindness in this as in other things, and actuated by that fervent love towards it, which is so natural to a man, who views it in the native soil of himself and his progenitors for several generations; I anticipate with pleasing expectation that retreat, in which I promise myself to realize, without alloy, the sweet enjoyment of partaking, in the midst of my fellow-citizens, the benign influence of good laws under a free government, the ever favorite object of my heart, and the happy reward, as I trust, of our mutual cares, labors, and dangers.

George Washington
United States - September 17, 1796

Abraham Lincoln's Gettysburg Address (19 November 1863)

Delivered at Gettysburg, Pennsylvania

"Four score and seven years ago our fathers brought forth on this continent a new nation, conceived in liberty, and dedicated to the proposition that all men are created equal.

"Now we are engaged in a great civil war, testing whether that nation, or any nation so conceived and so dedicated, can long endure. We are met on a great battlefield of that war. We have come to dedicate a portion of that field as a final resting place for those who here gave their lives that that nation might live. It is altogether fitting and proper that we should do this.

"But in a larger sense we cannot dedicate, we cannot consecrate, we cannot hallow this ground. The brave men, living and dead, who struggled here have consecrated it, far above our poor power to add or detract. The world will little note, nor long remember, what we say here, but it can never forget what they did here. It is for us the living, rather, to be dedicated here to the unfinished work which they who fought here have thus far so nobly advanced. It is rather for us to be here dedicated to the great task remaining before us,that from these honored dead we take increased devotion to that cause for which they gave the last full measure of devotion, that we here highly resolve that these dead shall not have died in vain, that this nation, under God, shall have a new birth of freedom, and that government of the people, by the people, for the people, shall not perish from the earth."

Abraham Lincoln's Second Inaugural Address (March 4, 1865)

Fellow countrymen:

At this second appearing to take the oath of the presidential office, there is less occasion for an extended address than there was at the first. Then a statement, somewhat in detail, of a course to be pursued, seemed fitting and proper. Now, at the expiration of four years, during which public declarations have been constantly called forth on every point and phase of the great contest which still absorbs the attention and engrosses the energies of the nation, little that is new could be presented. The progress of our arms, upon which all else chiefly depends, is as well known to the public as to myself; and it is, I trust, reasonably satisfactory and encouraging to all. With high hope for the future, no prediction in regard to it is ventured.

On the occasion corresponding to this four years ago, all thoughts were anxiously directed to an impending civil war. All dreaded it-- all sought to avert it. While the inaugural address was being delivered from this place, devoted altogether to saving the Union without war, insurgent agents were in the city seeking to destroy it without war-- seeking to dissolve the Union, and divide effects, by negotiation. Both parties deprecated war; but one of them would make war rather than let the nation survive; and the other would accept war rather than let it perish. And the war came.

One-eighth of the whole population were colored slaves, not distributed generally over the Union, but localized in the Southern part of it. These slaves constituted a peculiar and powerful interest. All knew that this interest was, somehow, the cause of the war. To strengthen, perpetuate, and extend this interest was the object for which the insurgents would rend the Union, even by war; while the government claimed no right to do more than to restrict the territorial enlargement of it.

Neither party expected for the war the magnitude or the duration which it has already attained. Neither anticipated that the cause of the conflict might cease with, or even before, the conflict itself should cease. Each looked for an easier triumph, and a result less fundamental and astounding. Both read the same Bible, and pray to the same God; and each invokes his aid against the other. It may seem strange that any men should dare to ask a just God's assistance in wringing their bread from the sweat of other men's faces; but let us judge not, that we be not judged. The prayers of both could not be answered-- that of neither has been answered fully.

The Almighty has his own purposes. "Woe unto the world because of offenses! for it must needs be that offenses come; but woe to that man by whom the offense cometh." If we shall suppose that American slavery is one of those offenses which, in the providence of God, must needs come, but which, having continued through his appointed time, he now wills to remove, and that he gives to both North and South this terrible war, as the woe due to those by whom the offense came, shall we discern therein any departure from those divine attributes which the believers in a living God always ascribe to him? Fondly do we hope--fervently do we pray--that this mighty scourge of war may speedily pass away. Yet, if God wills that it continue until all the wealth piled by the bondsman's two hundred and fifty years of unrequited toil shall be sunk, and until every drop of blood drawn by the lash shall be paid by another drawn with the sword, as was said three thousand years ago, so still it must be said, "The judgments of the Lord are true and righteous altogether."

With malice toward none; with charity for all; with firmness in the right, as God gives us to see the right, let us strive on to finish the work we are in; to bind up the nation's wounds; to care for him who shall have borne the battle, and for his widow, and his orphan--to do all which may achieve and cherish a just and lasting peace among ourselves, and with all nations.

Franklin D. Roosevelt's Acceptance Speech for His Renomination as Candidate for the Office of the Presidency, Philadelphia, Pennsylvania.

To see and listen to the on air broadcast of this speech, go to:

President Franklin Delano Roosevelt addresses the Democratic National Convention / 1936
https://www.youtube.com/watch?v=PXeWuDIMJj8

June 27, 1936

Senator Robinson, Members of the Democratic Convention, my friends:

Here, and in every community throughout the land, we are met at a time of great moment to the future of the Nation. It is an occasion to be dedicated to the simple and sincere expression of an attitude toward problems, the determination of which will profoundly affect America.

I come not only as a leader of a party, not only as a candidate for high office, but as one upon whom many critical hours have imposed and still impose a grave responsibility.

For the sympathy, help and confidence with which Americans have sustained me in my task I am grateful. For their loyalty I salute the members of our great party, in and out of political life in every part of the Union. I salute those of other parties, especially those in the Congress of the United States who on so many occasions have put partisanship aside. I thank the Governors of the several States, their Legislatures, their State and local officials who participated unselfishly and regardless of party in our efforts to achieve recovery and destroy abuses. Above all I thank the millions of Americans who have borne disaster bravely and have dared to smile through the storm.

America will not forget these recent years, will not forget that the rescue was not a mere party task. It was the concern of all of us. In our strength we rose together, rallied our energies together, applied the old rules of common sense, and together survived.

In those days we feared fear. That was why we fought fear. And today, my friends, we have won against the most dangerous of our foes. We have conquered fear.

But I cannot, with candor, tell you that all is well with the world. Clouds of suspicion, tides of ill-will and intolerance gather darkly in many places. In our own land we enjoy indeed a fullness of life greater than that of most Nations. But the rush of modern civilization itself has raised for us new difficulties, new problems which must be solved if we are to preserve to the United States the political and economic freedom for which Washington and Jefferson planned and fought.

Philadelphia is a good city in which to write American history. This is fitting ground on which to reaffirm the faith of our fathers; to pledge ourselves to restore to the people a wider freedom; to give to 1936 as the founders gave to 1776—an American way of life.

That very word freedom, in itself and of necessity, suggests freedom from some restraining power. In 1776 we sought freedom from the tyranny of a political autocracy—from the eighteenth century royalists who held special privileges from the crown. It was to perpetuate their privilege that they governed without the consent of the governed; that they denied the right of free assembly and free speech; that they restricted the worship of God; that they put the average man's property and the average man's life in pawn to the mercenaries of dynastic power; that they regimented the people.

And so it was to win freedom from the tyranny of political autocracy that the American Revolution was fought. That victory gave the business of governing into the hands of the average man, who won the right with his neighbors to make and order his own destiny through his own Government. Political tyranny was wiped out at Philadelphia on July 4, 1776.

Since that struggle, however, man's inventive genius released new forces in our land which reordered the lives of our people.. The age of machinery, of railroads; of steam and electricity; the telegraph and the radio; mass production, mass distribution—all of these combined to bring forward a new civilization and with it a new problem for those who sought to remain free.

For out of this modern civilization economic royalists carved new dynasties. New kingdoms were built upon concentration of control over material things. Through new uses of corporations, banks and securities, new machinery of industry and agriculture, of labor and capital—all undreamed of by the fathers—the whole structure of modern life was impressed into this royal service.

There was no place among this royalty for our many thousands of small business men and merchants who sought to make a worthy use of the American system of initiative and profit. They were no more free than the worker or the farmer. Even honest and progressive-minded men of wealth, aware of their obligation to their generation, could never know just where they fitted into this dynastic scheme of things.

It was natural and perhaps human that the privileged princes of these new economic dynasties, thirsting for power, reached out for control over Government itself. They created a new despotism and wrapped it in the robes of legal sanction. In its service new mercenaries sought to regiment the people, their labor, and their property. And as a result the average man once more confronts the problem that faced the Minute Man.

The hours men and women worked, the wages they received, the conditions of their labor—these had passed beyond the control of the people, and were imposed by this new industrial dictatorship. The savings of the average family, the capital of the small business man, the investments set aside for old age—other people's money—these were tools which the new economic royalty used to dig itself in.

Those who tilled the soil no longer reaped the rewards which were their right. The small measure of their gains was decreed by men in distant cities.

Throughout the Nation, opportunity was limited by monopoly. Individual initiative was crushed in the cogs of a great machine. The field open for free business was more and more restricted. Private enterprise, indeed, became too private. It became privileged enterprise, not free enterprise.

An old English judge once said: "Necessitous men are not free men." Liberty requires opportunity to make a living—a living decent according to the standard of the time, a living which gives man not only enough to live by, but something to live for.

For too many of us the political equality we once had won was meaningless in the face of economic inequality. A small group had concentrated into their own hands an almost complete control over other people's property, other people's money, other people's labor—other people's lives. For too many of us life was no longer free; liberty no longer real; men could no longer follow the pursuit of happiness.

Against economic tyranny such as this, the American citizen could appeal only to the organized power of Government. The collapse of 1929 showed up the despotism for what it was. The election of 1932 was the people's mandate to end it. Under that mandate it is being ended.

The royalists of the economic order have conceded that political freedom was the business of the Government, but they have maintained that economic slavery was nobody's business. They granted that the Government could protect the citizen in his right to vote, but they denied that the Government could do anything to protect the citizen in his right to work and his right to live.

Today we stand committed to the proposition that freedom is no half-and-half affair. If the average citizen is guaranteed equal opportunity in the polling place, he must have equal opportunity in the market place.

These economic royalists complain that we seek to overthrow the institutions of America. What they really complain of is that we seek to take away their power. Our allegiance to American institutions requires the overthrow of this kind of power. In vain they seek to hide behind the Flag and the Constitution. In their blindness they forget what the Flag and the Constitution stand for. Now, as always, they stand for democracy, not tyranny; for freedom, not subjection; and against a dictatorship by mob rule and the over-privileged alike.

The brave and clear platform adopted by this Convention, to which I heartily subscribe, sets forth that Government in a modern civilization has certain inescapable obligations to its citizens, among which are protection of the family and the home, the establishment of a democracy of opportunity, and aid to those overtaken by disaster.

But the resolute enemy within our gates is ever ready to beat down our words unless in greater courage we will fight for them.

For more than three years we have fought for them. This Convention, in every word and deed, has pledged that that fight will go on.

The defeats and victories of these years have given to us as a people a new understanding of our Government and of ourselves. Never since the early days of the New England town meeting have the affairs of Government been so widely discussed and so clearly appreciated. It has been brought home to us that the only effective guide for the safety of this most worldly of worlds, the greatest guide of all, is moral principle.

We do not see faith, hope and charity as unattainable ideals, but we use them as stout supports of a Nation fighting the fight for freedom in a modern civilization.

Faith— in the soundness of democracy in the midst of dictatorships.

Hope—renewed because we know so well the progress we have made.

Charity— in the true spirit of that grand old word. For charity literally translated from the original means love, the love that understands, that does not merely share the wealth of the giver, but in true sympathy and wisdom helps men to help themselves.

We seek not merely to make Government a mechanical implement, but to give it the vibrant personal character that is the very embodiment of human charity.

We are poor indeed if this Nation cannot afford to lift from every recess of American life the dread fear of the unemployed that they are not needed in the world. We cannot afford to accumulate a deficit in the books of human fortitude.

In the place of the palace of privilege we seek to build a temple out of faith and hope and charity.

It is a sobering thing, my friends, to be a servant of this great cause. We try in our daily work to remember that the cause belongs not to us, but to the people. The standard is not in the hands of you and me alone. It is carried by America. We seek daily to profit from experience, to learn to do better as our task proceeds.

Governments can err, Presidents do make mistakes, but the immortal Dante tells us that divine justice weighs the sins of the cold-blooded and the sins of the warm-hearted in different scales.

Better the occasional faults of a Government that lives in a spirit of charity than the consistent omissions of a Government frozen in the ice of its own indifference.

There is a mysterious cycle in human events. To some generations much is given. Of other generations much is expected. This generation of Americans has a rendezvous with destiny.

In this world of ours in other lands, there are some people, who, in times past, have lived and fought for freedom, and seem to have grown too weary to carry on the fight. They have sold their heritage of freedom for the illusion of a living. They have yielded their democracy.

I believe in my heart that only our success can stir their ancient hope. They begin to know that here in America we are waging a great and successful war. It is not alone a war against want and destitution and economic demoralization. It is more than that; it is a war for the survival of democracy. We are fighting to save a great and precious form of government for ourselves and for the world.

I accept the commission you have tendered me. I join with you. I am enlisted for the duration of the war.

President Dwight D. Eisenhower's Farewell Address (17 January 1961)

To see and listen to the on air broadcast of this speech, go to:

President Dwight David Eisenhower's Farewell Address
https://www.youtube.com/watch?v=OyBNmecVtdU

My fellow Americans:

Three days from now, after half a century in the service of our country, I shall lay down the responsibilities of office as, in traditional and solemn ceremony, the authority of the Presidency is vested in my successor.

This evening I come to you with a message of leave-taking and farewell, and to share a few final thoughts with you, my countrymen.

Like every other citizen, I wish the new President, and all who will labor with him, Godspeed. I pray that the coming years will be blessed with peace and prosperity for all.

Our people expect their President and the Congress to find essential agreement on issues of great moment, the wise resolution of which will better shape the future of the Nation.

My own relations with the Congress, which began on a remote and tenuous basis when, long ago, a member of the Senate appointed me to West Point, have since ranged to the intimate during the war and immediate post-war period, and, finally, to the mutually interdependent during these past eight years.

In this final relationship, the Congress and the Administration have, on most vital issues, cooperated well, to serve the national good rather than mere partisanship, and so have assured that the business of the Nation should go forward. So, my official relationship with the Congress ends in a feeling, on my part, of gratitude that we have been able to do so much together.

******

We now stand ten years past the midpoint of a century that has witnessed four major wars among great nations. Three of these involved our own country. Despite these holocausts America is today the strongest, the most influential and most productive nation in the world. Understandably proud of this pre-eminence, we yet realize that America's leadership and prestige depend, not merely upon our unmatched material progress, riches and military strength, but on how we use our power in the interests of world peace and human betterment.

******

Throughout America's adventure in free government, our basic purposes have been to keep the peace; to foster progress in human achievement, and to enhance liberty, dignity and integrity among people and among nations. To strive for less would be unworthy of a free and religious people. Any failure traceable to arrogance, or our lack of comprehension or readiness to sacrifice would inflict upon us grievous hurt both at home and abroad.

Progress toward these noble goals is persistently threatened by the conflict now engulfing the world. It commands our whole attention, absorbs our very beings. We face a hostile ideology-global in scope, atheistic in character, ruthless in purpose, and insidious in method. Unhappily the danger it poses promises to be of indefinite duration. To meet it successfully, there is called for, not so much the emotional and transitory sacrifices of crisis, but rather those which enable us to carry forward steadily, surely, and without complaint the burdens of a prolonged and complex struggle-with liberty at stake. Only thus shall we remain, despite every provocation, on our charted course toward permanent peace and human betterment.

Crises there will continue to be. In meeting them, whether foreign or domestic, great or small, there is a recurring temptation to feel that some spectacular and costly action could become the miraculous solution to all current difficulties. A huge increase in newer elements of our defense; development of unrealistic programs to cure every ill in agriculture; a dramatic expansion in basic and applied research- these and many other possibilities, each possibly promising in itself, may be suggested as the only way to the road we wish to travel.

But each proposal must be weighed in the light of a broader consideration: the need to maintain balance in and among national programs-balance between the private and the public economy, balance between cost and hoped for advantage-balance between the clearly necessary and the comfortably desirable; balance between our essential requirements as a nation and the duties imposed by the nation upon the individual; balance between action of the moment and the national welfare of the future. Good judgment seeks balance and progress; lack of it eventually finds imbalance and frustration.

The record of many decades stands as proof that our people and their government have, in the main, understood these truths and have responded to them well, in the face of stress and threat. But threats, new in kind or degree, constantly arise. I mention two only.

******

A vital element in keeping the peace is our military establishment. Our arms must be mighty, ready for instant action, so that no potential aggressor may be tempted to risk his own destruction.

Our military organization today bears little relation to that known by any of my predecessors in peace time, or indeed by the fighting men of World War II or Korea.

Until the latest of our world conflicts, the United States had no armaments industry. American makers of plowshares could, with time and as required, make swords as well. But now we can no longer risk emergency improvisation of national defense; we have been compelled to create a permanent armaments industry of vast proportions. Added to this, three and a half million men and women are directly engaged in the defense establishment. We annually spend on military security more than the net income of all United State corporations.

This conjunction of an immense military establishment and a large arms industry is new in the American experience. The total influence-economic, political, even spiritual-is felt in every city, every state house, every office of the Federal government. We recognize the imperative need for this development. Yet we must not fail to comprehend its grave implications. Our toil, resources and livelihood are all involved; so is the very structure of our society.

In the councils of government, we must guard against the acquisition of unwarranted influence, whether sought or unsought, by the military-industrial complex. The potential for the disastrous rise of misplaced power exists and will persist.

We must never let the weight of this combination endanger our liberties or democratic processes. We should take nothing for granted only an alert and knowledgeable citizenry can compel the proper meshing of the huge industrial and military machinery of defense with our peaceful methods and goals, so that security and liberty may prosper together.

Akin to, and largely responsible for the sweeping changes in our industrial-military posture, has been the technological revolution during recent decades.

In this revolution, research has become central; it also becomes more formalized, complex, and costly. A steadily increasing share is conducted for, by, or at the direction of, the Federal government.

Today, the solitary inventor, tinkering in his shop, has been over shadowed by task forces of scientists in laboratories and testing fields. In the same fashion, the free university, historically the fountainhead of free ideas and scientific discovery, has experienced a revolution in the conduct of research. Partly because of the huge costs involved, a government contract becomes virtually a substitute for intellectual curiosity. For every old blackboard there are now hundreds of new electronic computers.

The prospect of domination of the nation's scholars by Federal employment, project allocations, and the power of money is ever present and is gravely to be regarded.

Yet, in holding scientific research and discovery in respect, as we should, we must also be alert to the equal and opposite danger that public policy could itself become the captive of a scientific-technological elite.

It is the task of statesmanship to mold, to balance, and to integrate these and other forces, new and old, within the principles of our democratic system-ever aiming toward the supreme goals of our free society.

******

Another factor in maintaining balance involves the element of time. As we peer into society's future, we- you and I, and our government-must avoid the impulse to live only for today, plundering, for our own ease and convenience, the precious resources of tomorrow. We cannot mortgage the material assets of our grandchildren without risking the loss also of their political and spiritual heritage. We want democracy to survive for all generations to come, not to become the insolvent phantom of tomorrow.

******

Down the long lane of the history yet to be written America knows that this world of ours, ever growing smaller, must avoid becoming a community of dreadful fear and hate, and be, instead, a proud confederation of mutual trust and respect.

Such a confederation must be one of equals. The weakest must come to the conference table with the same confidence as do we, protected as we are by our moral, economic, and military strength. That table, though scarred by many past frustrations, cannot be abandoned for the certain agony of the battlefield.

Disarmament, with mutual honor and confidence, is a continuing imperative. Together we must learn how to compose difference, not with arms, but with intellect and decent purpose. Because this need is so sharp and apparent I confess that I lay down my official responsibilities in this field with a definite sense of disappointment. As one who has witnessed the horror and the lingering sadness of war-as one who knows that another war could utterly destroy this civilization which has been so slowly and painfully built over thousands of years-I wish I could say tonight that a lasting peace is in sight.

Happily, I can say that war has been avoided. Steady progress toward our ultimate goal has been made. But, so much remains to be done. As a private citizen, I shall never cease to do what little I can to help the world advance along that road.

******

So-in this my last good night to you as your President-I thank you for the many opportunities you have given me for public service in war and peace. I trust that in that service you find somethings worthy; as for the rest of it, I know you will find ways to improve performance in the future.

You and I-my fellow citizens-need to be strong in our faith that all nations, under God, will reach the goal of peace with justice. May we be ever unswerving in devotion to principle, confident but humble with power, diligent in pursuit of the Nation's great goals.

To all the peoples of the world, I once more give expression to America's prayerful and continuing inspiration:

We pray that peoples of all faiths, all races, all nations, may have their great human needs satisfied; that those now denied opportunity shall come to enjoy it to the full; that all who yearn for freedom may experience its spiritual blessings; that those who have freedom will understand, also, its heavy responsibilities; that all who are insensitive to the needs of others will learn charity; that the scourges of poverty, disease and ignorance will be made to disappear from the earth, and that, in the goodness of time, all peoples will come to live together in a peace guaranteed by the binding force of mutual respect and love.

President John F. Kennedy's Inaugural Address (20 January 1961)

To see and listen to the on air broadcast of this speech, go to:

President John Fitzgerald Kennedy's Inaugural Address / January 20th 1961
https://www.youtube.com/watch?app=desktop&v=njE7raNnRrY

Vice President Johnson, Mr. Speaker, Mr. Chief Justice, President Eisenhower, Vice President Nixon, President Truman, Reverend Clergy, fellow citizens:

We observe today not a victory of party but a celebration of freedom--symbolizing an end as well as a beginning--signifying renewal as well as change. For I have sworn before you and Almighty God the same solemn oath our forbears prescribed nearly a century and three-quarters ago.

The world is very different now. For man holds in his mortal hands the power to abolish all forms of human poverty and all forms of human life. And yet the same revolutionary beliefs for which our forebears fought are still at issue around the globe--the belief that the rights of man come not from the generosity of the state but from the hand of God.

We dare not forget today that we are the heirs of that first revolution. Let the word go forth from this time and place, to friend and foe alike, that the torch has been passed to a new generation of Americans--born in this century, tempered by war, disciplined by a hard and bitter peace, proud of our ancient heritage--and unwilling to witness or permit the slow undoing of those human rights to which this nation has always been committed, and to which we are committed today at home and around the world.

Let every nation know, whether it wishes us well or ill, that we shall pay any price, bear any burden, meet any hardship, support any friend, oppose any foe to assure the survival and the success of liberty.

This much we pledge--and more.

To those old allies whose cultural and spiritual origins we share, we pledge the loyalty of faithful friends. United there is little we cannot do in a host of cooperative ventures. Divided there is little we can do--for we dare not meet a powerful challenge at odds and split asunder.

To those new states whom we welcome to the ranks of the free, we pledge our word that one form of colonial control shall not have passed away merely to be replaced by a far more iron tyranny. We shall not always expect to find them supporting our view. But we shall always hope to find them strongly supporting their own freedom--and to remember that, in the past, those who foolishly sought power by riding the back of the tiger ended up inside.

To those people in the huts and villages of half the globe struggling to break the bonds of mass misery, we pledge our best efforts to help them help themselves, for whatever period is required--not because the communists may be doing it, not because we seek their votes, but because it is right. If a free society cannot help the many who are poor, it cannot save the few who are rich.

To our sister republics south of our border, we offer a special pledge--to convert our good words into good deeds--in a new alliance for progress--to assist free men and free governments in casting off the chains of poverty. But this peaceful revolution of hope cannot become the prey of hostile powers. Let all our neighbors know that we shall join with them to oppose aggression or subversion anywhere in the Americas. And let every other power know that this Hemisphere intends to remain the master of its own house.

To that world assembly of sovereign states, the United Nations, our last best hope in an age where the instruments of war have far outpaced the instruments of peace, we renew our pledge of support--to prevent it from becoming merely a forum for invective--to strengthen its shield of the new and the weak--and to enlarge the area in which its writ may run.

Finally, to those nations who would make themselves our adversary, we offer not a pledge but a request: that both sides begin anew the quest for peace, before the dark powers of destruction unleashed by science engulf all humanity in planned or accidental self-destruction.

We dare not tempt them with weakness. For only when our arms are sufficient beyond doubt can we be certain beyond doubt that they will never be employed.

But neither can two great and powerful groups of nations take comfort from our present course--both sides overburdened by the cost of modern weapons, both rightly alarmed by the steady spread of the deadly atom, yet both racing to alter that uncertain balance of terror that stays the hand of mankind's final war.

So let us begin anew--remembering on both sides that civility is not a sign of weakness, and sincerity is always subject to proof. Let us never negotiate out of fear. But let us never fear to negotiate.

Let both sides explore what problems unite us instead of belaboring those problems which divide us. Let

both sides, for the first time, formulate serious and precise proposals for the inspection and control of arms--and bring the absolute power to destroy other nations under the absolute control of all nations.

Let both sides seek to invoke the wonders of science instead of its terrors. Together let us explore the stars, conquer the deserts, eradicate disease, tap the ocean depths and encourage the arts and commerce.

Let both sides unite to heed in all corners of the earth the command of Isaiah--to "undo the heavy burdens . . . (and) let the oppressed go free."

And if a beachhead of cooperation may push back the jungle of suspicion, let both sides join in creating a new endeavor, not a new balance of power, but a new world of law, where the strong are just and the weak secure and the peace preserved.

All this will not be finished in the first one hundred days. Nor will it be finished in the first one thousand days, nor in the life of this Administration, nor even perhaps in our lifetime on this planet. But let us begin.

In your hands, my fellow citizens, more than mine, will rest the final success or failure of our course. Since this country was founded, each generation of Americans has been summoned to give testimony to its national loyalty. The graves of young Americans who answered the call to service surround the globe.

Now the trumpet summons us again--not as a call to bear arms, though arms we need--not as a call to battle, though embattled we are-- but a call to bear the burden of a long twilight struggle, year in and year out, "rejoicing in hope, patient in tribulation"--a struggle against the common enemies of man: tyranny, poverty, disease and war itself.

Can we forge against these enemies a grand and global alliance, North and South, East and West, that can assure a more fruitful life for all mankind? Will you join in that historic effort?

In the long history of the world, only a few generations have been granted the role of defending freedom in its hour of maximum danger. I do not shrink from this responsibility--I welcome it. I do not believe that any of us would exchange places with any other people or any other generation. The energy, the faith, the devotion which we bring to this endeavor will light our country and all who serve it--and the glow from that fire can truly light the world.

And so, my fellow Americans: ask not what your country can do for you--ask what you can do for your country.

My fellow citizens of the world: ask not what America will do for you, but what together we can do for the freedom of man.

Finally, whether you are citizens of America or citizens of the world, ask of us here the same high standards of strength and sacrifice which we ask of you. With a good conscience our only sure reward, with history the final judge of our deeds, let us go forth to lead the land we love, asking His blessing and His help, but knowing that here on earth God's work must truly be our own.

JFK Address At Rice University / September 12th 1962

To see and listen to the on air broadcast of this speech, go to:

President John F. Kennedy Address at Rice University on the Space Effort
https://www.youtube.com/watch?v=WZyRbnpGyzQ

President Pitzer, Mr. Vice President, Governor, Congressman Thomas, Senator Wiley, and Congressman Miller, Mr. Webb. Mr. Bell, scientists, distinguished guests, and ladies and gentlemen:

I appreciate your president having made me an honorary visiting professor, and I will assure you that my first lecture will be very brief. I am delighted to be here and I'm particularly delighted to be here on this occasion.

We meet at a college noted for knowledge, in a city noted for progress, in a State noted for strength, and we stand in need of all three, for we meet in an hour of change and challenge, in a decade of hope and fear, in an age of both knowledge and ignorance. The greater our knowledge increases, the greater our ignorance unfolds.

Despite the striking fact that most of the scientists that the world has ever known are alive and working today, despite the fact that this Nation's own scientific manpower is doubling every 12 years in a rate of growth more than three times that of our population as a whole, despite that, the vast stretches of the unknown and the unanswered and the unfinished still far out-strip our collective comprehension.

No man can fully grasp how far and how fast we have come, but condense, if you will, the 50,000 years of man's recorded history in a time span of but a half century. Stated in these terms, we know very little about the first 40 years, except at the end of them advanced man had learned to use the skins of animals to cover them. Then about 10 years ago, under this standard, man emerged from his caves to construct other kinds of shelter. Only 5 years ago man learned to write and use a cart with wheels. Christianity began less than 2 years ago. The printing press came this year, and then less than 2 months ago, during this whole 50-year span of human history, the steam engine provided a new source of power.

Newton explored the meaning of gravity. Last month electric lights and telephones and automobiles and airplanes became available. Only last week did we develop penicillin and television and nuclear power, and now if America's new spacecraft succeeds in reaching Venus, we will have literally reached the stars before midnight tonight.

This is a breathtaking pace, and such a pace cannot help but create new ills as it dispels old, new ignorance, new problems, new dangers. Surely the opening vistas of space promise high costs and hardships, as well as high reward.

So it is not surprising that some would have us stay where we are a little longer to rest, to wait. But this city of Houston, this State of Texas, this country of the United States was not built by those who waited and rested and wished to look behind them. This country was conquered by those who moved forward- and so will space.

William Bradford, speaking in 1630 of the founding of the Plymouth Bay Colony, said that all great and honorable actions are accompanied with great difficulties, and both must be enterprised and overcome with answerable courage.

If this capsule history of our progress teaches us anything, it is that man, in his quest for knowledge and progress, is determined and cannot be deterred. The exploration of space will go ahead, whether we join in it or not, and it is one of the great adventures of all time, and no nation which expects to be the leader of other nations can expect to stay behind in this race for space.

Those who came before us made certain that this country rode the first waves of the industrial revolutions, the first waves of modern invention, and the first wave of nuclear power, and this generation does not intend to founder in the backwash of the coming age of space. We mean to be a part of it - we mean to lead it. For the eyes of the world now look into space, to the moon and to the planets beyond, and we have vowed that we shall not see it governed by a hostile flag of conquest, but by a banner of freedom and peace. We have vowed that we shall not see space filled with weapons of mass destruction, but with instruments of knowledge and understanding.

Yet the vows of this Nation can only be fulfilled if we in this Nation are first, and, therefore, we intend to be first. In short, our leadership in science and in industry, our hopes for peace and security, our obligations to ourselves as well as others, all require us to make this effort, to solve these mysteries, to solve them for the good of all men, and to become the world's leading space-faring nation.

We set sail on this new sea because there is new knowledge to be gained, and new rights to be won, and they must be won and used for the progress of all people. For space science, like nuclear science and all technology, has no conscience of its own. Whether it will become a force for good or ill depends on man, and only if the United States occupies a position of pre-eminence can we help decide whether this new ocean will be a sea of peace or a new terrifying theater of war. I do not say that we should or will go unprotected against the hostile misuse of space any more than we go unprotected against the hostile use of land or sea, but I do say that space can be explored and mastered without feeding the fires of war, without repeating the mistakes that man has made in extending his writ around this globe of ours.

There is no strife, no prejudice, no national conflict in outer space as yet. Its hazards are hostile to us all. Its conquest deserves the best of all mankind, and its opportunity for peaceful cooperation may never come again. But why, some say, the moon? Why choose this as our goal? And they may well ask why climb the highest mountain. Why, 35 years ago, fly the Atlantic? Why does Rice play Texas?
We choose to go to the moon. We choose to go to the moon in this decade and do the other things, not because they are easy, but because they are hard, because that goal will serve to organize and measure the best of our energies and skills, because that challenge is one that we are willing to accept, one we are unwilling to postpone, and one which we intend to win, and the others, too.

It is for these reasons that I regard the decision last year to shift our efforts in space from low to high gear as among the most important decisions that will be made during my incumbency in the Office of the Presidency.

In the last 24 hours we have seen facilities now being created for the greatest and most complex exploration in man's history. We have felt the ground shake and the air shattered by the testing of a Saturn C-1 booster rocket, many times as powerful as the Atlas which launched John Glenn, generating power equivalent to 10,000 automobiles with their accelerators on the floor. We have seen the site where five F-1 rocket engines, each one as powerful as all eight engines of the Saturn combined, will be clustered together to make the advanced Saturn missile, assembled in a new building to be built at Cape Canaveral as tall as a 48-story structure, as wide as a city block, and as long as two lengths of this field.

Within these last 19 months at least 45 satellites have circled the earth. Some 40 of them were "made in the United States of America" and they were far more sophisticated and supplied far more knowledge to the people of the world than those of the Soviet Union.

The Mariner spacecraft now on its way to Venus is the most intricate instrument in the history of space science. The accuracy of that shot is comparable to firing a missile from Cape Canaveral and dropping it in this stadium between the 40-yard lines.

Transit satellites are helping our ships at sea to steer a safer course. Tiros satellites have given us unprecedented warnings of hurricanes and storms, and will do the same for forest fires and icebergs. We have had our failures, but so have others, even if they do not admit them. And they may be less public.

To be sure, we are behind, and will be behind for some time in manned flight. But we do not intend to stay behind, and in this decade we shall make up and move ahead.

The growth of our science and education will be enriched by new knowledge of our universe and environment, by new techniques of learning and mapping and observation, by new tools and computers for industry, medicine, the home as well as the school. Technical institutions, such as Rice, will reap the harvest of these gains.

And finally, the space effort itself, while still in its infancy, has already created a great number of new companies, and tens of thousands of new jobs. Space and related industries are generating new demands in investment and skilled personnel, and this city and this State, and this region, will share greatly in this growth. What was once the furthest outpost on the old frontier of the West will be the furthest outpost on the new frontier of science and space. Houston, your City of Houston, with its Manned Spacecraft Center, will become the heart of a large scientific and engineering community. During the next 5 years the National Aeronautics and Space Administration expects to double the number of scientists and engineers in this area, to increase its outlays for salaries and expenses to $60 million a year; to invest some $200 million in plant and laboratory facilities; and to direct or contract for new space efforts over $1 billion from this Center in this City.

To be sure, all this costs us all a good deal of money. This year's space budget is three times what it was in January 1961, and it is greater than the space budget of the previous 8 years combined. That budget now stands at $5,400 million a year-a staggering sum, though somewhat less than we pay for cigarettes and cigars every year. Space expenditures will soon rise some more from 40 cents per person per week to more than 50 cents a week for every man, woman, and child in the United States, for we have given this program a high national priority even though I realize that this is in some measure an act of faith and vision, for we do not now know what benefits await us. But if I were to say, my fellow citizens, that we shall send to the moon, 240,000 miles away from the control station in Houston, a giant rocket more than 300 feet tall, the length of this football field, made of new metal alloys, some of which have not yet been invented, capable of standing heat and stresses several times more than have ever been experienced, fitted together with a precision better than the finest watch, carrying all the equipment needed for propulsion, guidance, control, communications, food and survival, on an untried mission, to an unknown celestial body, and then return it safely to earth, reentering the atmosphere at speeds of over 25,000 miles per hour, causing heat about half that of the temperature of the sun - almost as hot as it is here today - and do all this, and do it right, and do it first before this decade is out, then we must be bold.

I'm the one who is doing all the work, so we just want you to stay cool for a minute. [Laughter] However, I think we're going to do it, and I think that we must pay what needs to be paid. I don't think we ought to waste any money, but I think we ought to do the job. And this will be done in the decade of the sixties. It may be done while some of you are still here at school at this college and university. It will be done during the terms of office of some of the people who sit here on this platform. But it will be done. And it will be done before the end of this decade.

I am delighted that this university is playing a part in putting a man on the moon as part of a great national effort of the United States of America.

Many years ago the great British explorer George Mallory, who was to die on Mount Everest, was asked why did he want to climb it. He said, "Because it is there."

Well, space is there, and we're going to climb it, and the moon and the planets are there, and new hopes for knowledge and peace are there. And, therefore, as we set sail we ask God's blessing on the most hazardous and dangerous and greatest adventure on which man has ever embarked.
Thank you.

NOTE: The President spoke in the Rice University Stadium at 10 a.m.

Martin Luther King Jr.'s 'I Have a Dream' Speech / August 28th 1963

To see and listen to the on air broadcast of this speech, go to:

Martin Luther King's 'I Have A Dream' Speech
https://www.youtube.com/watch?v=smEqnnklfYs

Address to civil rights marchers by the Rev. Dr. Martin Luther King Jr. in Washington, D.C.

I am happy to join with you today in what will go down in history as the greatest demonstration for freedom in the history of our nation.

Five score years ago, a great American, in whose symbolic shadow we stand today, signed the Emancipation Proclamation. This momentous decree came as a great beacon light of hope to millions of Negro slaves who had been seared in the flames of withering injustice. It came as a joyous daybreak to end the long night of their captivity.

But 100 years later, the Negro still is not free. One hundred years later, the life of the Negro is still sadly crippled by the manacles of segregation and the chains of discrimination. One hundred years later, the Negro lives on a lonely island of poverty in the midst of a vast ocean of material prosperity. One hundred years later, the Negro is still languished in the corners of American society and finds himself an exile in his own land. And so we've come here today to dramatize a shameful condition.

In a sense we've come to our nation's capital to cash a check. When the architects of our republic wrote the magnificent words of the Constitution and the Declaration of Independence, they were signing a promissory note to which every American was to fall heir. This note was a promise that all men -- yes, black men as well as white men -- would be guaranteed the unalienable rights of life, liberty, and the pursuit of happiness.

It is obvious today that America has defaulted on this promissory note insofar as her citizens of color are concerned. Instead of honoring this sacred obligation, America has given the Negro people a bad check, a check that has come back marked "insufficient funds."

But we refuse to believe that the bank of justice is bankrupt. We refuse to believe that there are insufficient funds in the great vaults of opportunity of this nation. And so we've come to cash this check, a check that will give us upon demand the riches of freedom and security of justice. We have also come to his hallowed spot to remind America of the fierce urgency of now. This is no time to engage in the luxury of cooling off or to take the tranquilizing drug of gradualism. Now is the time to make real the promises of democracy. Now is the time to rise from the dark and desolate valley of segregation to the sunlit path of racial justice. Now is the time to lift our nation from the quicksands of racial injustice to the solid rock of brotherhood. Now is the time to make justice a reality for all of God's children.

It would be fatal for the nation to overlook the urgency of the moment. This sweltering summer of the Negro's legitimate discontent will not pass until there is an invigorating autumn of freedom and equality. 1963 is not an end but a beginning. Those who hoped that the Negro needed to blow off steam and will now be content will have a rude awakening if the nation returns to business as usual. There will be neither rest nor tranquility in America until the Negro is granted his citizenship rights. The whirlwinds of revolt will continue to shake the foundations of our nation until the bright day of justice emerges.

But there is something that I must say to my people who stand on the warm threshold which leads into the palace of justice. In the process of gaining our rightful place we must not be guilty of wrongful deeds. Let us not seek to satisfy our thirst for freedom by drinking from the cup of bitterness and hatred. We must forever conduct our struggle on the high plane of dignity and discipline. We must not allow our creative protest to degenerate into physical violence. Again and again we must rise to the majestic heights of meeting physical force with soul force. The marvelous new militancy which has engulfed the Negro community must not lead us to a distrust of all white people, for many of our white brothers, as evidenced by their presence here today, have come to realize that their destiny is tied up with our destiny. And they have come to realize that their freedom is inextricably bound to our freedom. We cannot walk alone.

As we walk, we must make the pledge that we shall always march ahead. We cannot turn back. There are those who are asking the devotees of civil rights, "When will you be satisfied?" We can never be satisfied as long as the Negro is the victim of the unspeakable horrors of police brutality. We can never be satisfied as long as our bodies, heavy with the fatigue of travel, cannot gain lodging in the motels of the highways and the hotels of the cities. We cannot be satisfied as long as the Negro's basic mobility is from a smaller ghetto to a larger one. We can never be satisfied as long as our children are stripped of their selfhood and robbed of their dignity by signs stating "for whites only." We cannot be satisfied as long as a Negro in Mississippi cannot vote and a Negro in New York believes he has nothing for which to vote. No, no we are not satisfied and we will not be satisfied until justice rolls down like waters and righteousness like a mighty stream.

I am not unmindful that some of you have come here out of great trials and tribulations. Some of you have come fresh from narrow jail cells. Some of you have come from areas where your quest for freedom left you battered by storms of persecution and staggered by the winds of police brutality. You have been the veterans of creative suffering. Continue to work with the faith that unearned suffering is redemptive.

Go back to Mississippi, go back to Alabama, go back to South Carolina, go back to Georgia, go back to Louisiana, go back to the slums and ghettos of our northern cities, knowing that somehow this situation can and will be changed.

Let us not wallow in the valley of despair. I say to you today my friends -- so even though we face the difficulties of today and tomorrow, I still have a dream. It is a dream deeply rooted in the American dream.

I have a dream that one day this nation will rise up and live out the true meaning of its creed: "We hold these truths to be self-evident, that all men are created equal."

I have a dream that one day on the red hills of Georgia the sons of former slaves and the sons of former slave owners will be able to sit down together at the table of brotherhood.

I have a dream that one day even the state of Mississippi, a state sweltering with the heat of injustice, sweltering with the heat of oppression, will be transformed into an oasis of freedom and justice.

I have a dream that my four little children will one day live in a nation where they will not be judged by the color of their skin but by the content of their character.
I have a dream today.

I have a dream that one day down in Alabama, with its vicious racists, with its governor having his lips dripping with the words of interposition and nullification -- one day right there in Alabama little black boys and black girls will be able to join hands with little white boys and white girls as sisters and brothers.

I have a dream today.

I have a dream that one day every valley shall be exalted, and every hill and mountain shall be made low, the rough places will be made plain, and the crooked places will be made straight, and the glory of the Lord shall be revealed and all flesh shall see it together.

This is our hope. This is the faith that I go back to the South with. With this faith we will be able to hew out of the mountain of despair a stone of hope. With this faith we will be able to transform the jangling discords of our nation into a beautiful symphony of brotherhood. With this faith we will be able to work together, to pray together, to struggle together, to go to jail together, to stand up for freedom together, knowing that we will be free one day.

This will be the day, this will be the day when all of God's children will be able to sing with new meaning "My country 'tis of thee, sweet land of liberty, of thee I sing. Land where my father's died, land of the Pilgrim's pride, from every mountainside, let freedom ring!"

And if America is to be a great nation, this must become true. And so let freedom ring from the prodigious hilltops of New Hampshire. Let freedom ring from the mighty mountains of New York. Let freedom ring from the heightening Alleghenies of Pennsylvania.

Let freedom ring from the snow-capped Rockies of Colorado. Let freedom ring from the curvaceous slopes of California.

But not only that; let freedom ring from Stone Mountain of Georgia. Let
freedom ring from Lookout Mountain of Tennessee.
Let freedom ring from every hill and molehill of Mississippi -- from every mountainside.

Let freedom ring. And when this happens, and when we allow freedom ring -- when we let it ring from every village and every hamlet, from every state and every city, we will be able to speed up that day when all of God's children -- black men and white men, Jews and Gentiles, Protestants and Catholics -- will be able to join hands and sing in the words of the old Negro spiritual: "Free at last! Free at last! Thank God Almighty, we are free at last!"

Barack Obama's Keynote Address at the 2004 DNC Convention / July 27th 2004

To see and listen to the on air broadcast of this speech, go to:

C-Span: Barack Obama's Keynote Address to the Democratic National Convention / 2004
https://www.youtube.com/watch?v=R9FJKQTJ3V4

On behalf of the great state of Illinois, crossroads of a nation, land of Lincoln, let me express my deep gratitude for the privilege of addressing this convention. Tonight is a particular honor for me because, let's face it, my presence on this stage is pretty unlikely. My father was a foreign student, born and raised in a small village in Kenya. He grew up herding goats, went to school in a tin-roof shack. His father, my grandfather, was a cook, a domestic servant.

But my grandfather had larger dreams for his son. Through hard work and perseverance my father got a scholarship to study in a magical place: America, which stood as a beacon of freedom and opportunity to so many who had come before. While studying here, my father met my mother. She was born in a town on the other side of the world, in Kansas. Her father worked on oil rigs and farms through most of the Depression. The day after Pearl Harbor he signed up for duty, joined Patton's army and marched across Europe. Back home, my grandmother raised their baby and went to work on a bomber assembly line. After the war, they studied on the GI Bill, bought a house through FHA, and moved west in search of opportunity.

And they, too, had big dreams for their daughter, a common dream, born of two continents. My parents shared not only an improbable love; they shared an abiding faith in the possibilities of this nation. They would give me an African name, Barack, or "blessed," believing that in a tolerant America your name is no barrier to success. They imagined me going to the best schools in the land, even though they weren't rich, because in a generous America you don't have to be rich to achieve your potential. They are both passed away now. Yet, I know that, on this night, they look down on me with pride.

I stand here today, grateful for the diversity of my heritage, aware that my parents' dreams live on in my precious daughters. I stand here knowing that my story is part of the larger American story, that I owe a debt to all of those who came before me, and that, in no other country on earth, is my story even possible. Tonight, we gather to affirm the greatness of our nation, not because of the height of our skyscrapers, or the power of our military, or the size of our economy. Our pride is based on a very simple premise, summed up in a declaration made over two hundred years ago, "We hold these truths to be self-evident, that all men are created equal. That they are endowed by their Creator with certain inalienable rights. That among these are life, liberty and the pursuit of happiness."

That is the true genius of America, a faith in the simple dreams of its people, the insistence on small miracles. That we can tuck in our children at night and know they are fed and clothed and safe from harm. That we can say what we think, write what we think, without hearing a sudden knock on the door. That we can have an idea and start our own business without paying a bribe or hiring somebody's son. That we can participate in the political process without fear of retribution, and that our votes will he counted - or at least, most of the time.

This year, in this election, we are called to reaffirm our values and commitments, to hold them against a hard reality and see how we are measuring up to the legacy of our forebearers and the promise of future generations. And fellow Americans - Democrats, Republicans, Independents - I say to you tonight: we have more work to do. More to do for the workers I met in Galesburg, Illinois who are losing their union jobs at the Maytag plant that's moving to Mexico and now are having to compete with their own children for jobs that pay seven bucks an hour.

More to do for the father I met who was losing his job and choking back tears, wondering how he would pay $4,500 a month for the drugs his son needs without the health benefits he counted on.

More to do for the young woman in East St. Louis, and thousands more like her, who has the grades, has the drive, has the will, but doesn't have the money to go to college

Don't get me wrong. The people I meet in small towns and big cities, in diners and office parks, they don't expect government to solve all their problems. They know they have to work hard to get ahead and they want to. Go into the collar counties around Chicago, and people will tell you they don't want their tax money wasted by a welfare agency or the Pentagon. Go into any inner city neighborhood, and folks will tell you that government alone can't teach kids to learn. They know that parents have to parent, that children can't achieve unless we raise their expectations and turn off the television sets and eradicate the slander that says a black youth with a book is acting white. No, people don't expect government to solve all their problems. But they sense, deep in their bones, that with just a change in priorities, we can make sure that every child in America has a decent shot at life, and that the doors of opportunity remain open to all. They know we can do better. And they want that choice.

In this election, we offer that choice. Our party has chosen a man to lead us who embodies the best this country has to offer. That man is John Kerry. John Kerry understands the ideals of community, faith, and sacrifice, because they've defined his life. From his heroic service in Vietnam to his years as prosecutor and lieutenant governor, through two decades in the United States Senate, he has devoted himself to this country. Again and again, we've seen him make tough choices when easier ones were available. His values and his record affirm what is best in us.

John Kerry believes in an America where hard work is rewarded. So instead of offering tax breaks to companies shipping jobs overseas, he'll offer them to companies creating jobs here at home. John Kerry believes in an America where all Americans can afford the same health coverage our politicians in Washington have for themselves. John Kerry believes in energy independence, so we aren't held hostage to the profits of oil companies or the sabotage of foreign oil fields. John Kerry believes in the constitutional freedoms that have made our country the envy of the world, and he will never sacrifice our basic liberties nor use faith as a wedge to divide us. And John Kerry believes that in a dangerous world, war must be an option, but it should never he the first option.

A while back, I met a young man named Shamus at the VFW Hall in East Moline, Illinois. He was a good-looking kid, six-two or six-three, clear-eyed, with an easy smile. He told me he'd joined the Marines and was heading to Iraq the following week. As I listened to him explain why he'd enlisted, his absolute faith in our country and its leaders, his devotion to duty and service, I thought this young man was all any of us might hope for in a child. But then I asked myself: Are we serving Shamus as well as he was serving us? I thought of more than 900 service men and women, sons and daughters, husbands and wives, friends and neighbors, who will not be returning to their hometowns. I thought of families I had met who were struggling to get by without a loved one's full income, or whose loved ones had returned with a limb missing or with nerves shattered, but who still lacked long-term health benefits because they were reservists. When we send our young men and women into harm's way, we have a solemn obligation not to fudge the numbers or shade the truth about why they're going, to care for their families while they're gone, to tend to the soldiers upon their return, and to never ever go to war without enough troops to win the war, secure the peace, and earn the respect of the world.

Now let me be clear. We have real enemies in the world. These enemies must be found. They must be pursued and they must be defeated. John Kerry knows this. And just as Lieutenant Kerry did not hesitate to risk his life to protect the men who served with him in Vietnam, President Kerry will not hesitate one moment to use our military might to keep America safe and secure. John Kerry believes in America. And he knows it's not enough for just some of us to prosper. For alongside our famous individualism, there's another ingredient in the American saga.

A belief that we are connected as one people. If there's a child on the south side of Chicago who can't read, that matters to me, even if it's not my child. If there's a senior citizen somewhere who can't pay for her prescription and has to choose between medicine and the rent, that makes my life poorer, even if it's not my grandmother. If there's an Arab American family being rounded up without benefit of an attorney or due process, that threatens my civil liberties. It's that fundamental belief - I am my brother's keeper, I am my sister's keeper - that makes this country work. It's what allows us to pursue our individual dreams, yet still come together as a single American family. "E pluribus unum."

Out of many, one.

Yet even as we speak, there are those who are preparing to divide us, the spin masters and negative ad peddlers who embrace the politics of anything goes. Well, I say to them tonight, there's not a liberal America and a conservative America - there's the United States of America. There's not a black America and white America and Latino America and Asian America; there's the United States of America. The pundits like to slice-and-dice our country into Red States and Blue States; Red States for Republicans, Blue States for Democrats. But I've got news for them, too. We worship an awesome God in the Blue States, and we don't like federal agents poking around our libraries in the Red States. We coach Little League in the Blue States and have gay friends in the Red States. There are patriots who opposed the war in Iraq and patriots who supported it. We are one people, all of us pledging allegiance to the stars and stripes, all of us defending the United States of America.

In the end, that's what this election is about. Do we participate in a politics of cynicism or a politics of hope? John Kerry calls on us to hope. John Edwards calls on us to hope. I'm not talking about blind optimism here - the almost willful ignorance that thinks unemployment will go away if we just don't talk about it, or the health care crisis will solve itself if we just ignore it. No, I'm talking about something more substantial. It's the hope of slaves sitting around a fire singing freedom songs; the hope of immigrants setting out for distant shores; the hope of a young naval lieutenant bravely patrolling the Mekong Delta; the hope of a millworker's son who dares to defy the odds; the hope of a skinny kid with a funny name who believes that America has a place for him, too. The audacity of hope!

In the end, that is God's greatest gift to us, the bedrock of this nation; the belief in things not seen; the belief that there are better days ahead. I believe we can give our middle class relief and provide working families with a road to opportunity. I believe we can provide jobs to the jobless, homes to the homeless, and reclaim young people in cities across America from violence and despair. I believe that as we stand on the crossroads of history, we can make the right choices, and meet the challenges that face us. America!

Tonight, if you feel the same energy I do, the same urgency I do, the same passion I do, the same hopefulness I do - if we do what we must do, then I have no doubt that all across the country, from Florida to Oregon, from Washington to Maine, the people will rise up in November, and John Kerry will be sworn in as president, and John Edwards will be sworn in as vice president, and this country will reclaim its promise, and out of this long political darkness a brighter day will come.
Thank you and God bless you.

Barack Obama's Inaugural Address / January 20th 2009

To see and listen to the on air broadcast of this speech, go to:

Barack Obama's Inaugural Address / January 20th 2009
https://www.youtube.com/watch?v=S4VoolvEsyQ

My fellow citizens: I stand here today humbled by the task before us, grateful for the trust you've bestowed, mindful of the sacrifices borne by our ancestors.

I thank President Bush for his service to our nation -- as well as the generosity and cooperation he has shown throughout this transition.

Forty-four Americans have now taken the presidential oath. The words have been spoken during rising tides of prosperity and the still waters of peace. Yet, every so often, the oath is taken amidst gathering clouds and raging storms. At these moments, America has carried on not simply because of the skill or vision of those in high office, but because we, the people, have remained faithful to the ideals of our forebears and true to our founding documents.

So it has been; so it must be with this generation of Americans.

That we are in the midst of crisis is now well understood. Our nation is at war against a far-reaching network of violence and hatred. Our economy is badly weakened, a consequence of greed and irresponsibility on the part of some, but also our collective failure to make hard choices and prepare the nation for a new age. Homes have been lost, jobs shed, businesses shuttered. Our health care is too costly, our schools fail too many -- and each day brings further evidence that the ways we use energy strengthen our adversaries and threaten our planet.

These are the indicators of crisis, subject to data and statistics. Less measurable, but no less profound, is a sapping of confidence across our land; a nagging fear that America's decline is inevitable, that the next generation must lower its sights.

Today I say to you that the challenges we face are real. They are serious and they are many. They will not be met easily or in a short span of time. But know this America: They will be met.

On this day, we gather because we have chosen hope over fear, unity of purpose over conflict and discord. On this day, we come to proclaim an end to the petty grievances and false promises, the recriminations and worn-out dogmas that for far too long have strangled our politics. We remain a young nation. But in the words of Scripture, the time has come to set aside childish things. The time has come to reaffirm our enduring spirit; to choose our better history; to carry forward that precious gift, that noble idea passed on from generation to generation: the God-given promise that all are equal, all are free, and all deserve a chance to pursue their full measure of happiness.

In reaffirming the greatness of our nation we understand that greatness is never a given. It must be earned. Our journey has never been one of short-cuts or settling for less. It has not been the path for the faint-hearted, for those that prefer leisure over work, or seek only the pleasures of riches and fame. Rather, it has been the risk-takers, the doers, the makers of things -- some celebrated, but more often men and women obscure in their labor -- who have carried us up the long rugged path towards prosperity and freedom.

For us, they packed up their few worldly possessions and traveled across oceans in search of a new life. For us, they toiled in sweatshops, and settled the West, endured the lash of the whip, and plowed the hard earth. For us, they fought and died in places like Concord and Gettysburg, Normandy and Khe Sahn.

Time and again these men and women struggled and sacrificed and worked till their hands were raw so that we might live a better life. They saw America as bigger than the sum of our individual ambitions, greater than all the differences of birth or wealth or faction.

This is the journey we continue today. We remain the most prosperous, powerful nation on Earth. Our workers are no less productive than when this crisis began. Our minds are no less inventive, our goods and services no less needed than they were last week, or last month, or last year. Our capacity remains undiminished. But our time of standing pat, of protecting narrow interests and putting off unpleasant decisions -- that time has surely passed. Starting today, we must pick ourselves up, dust ourselves off, and begin again the work of remaking America.

For everywhere we look, there is work to be done. The state of our economy calls for action, bold and swift. And we will act, not only to create new jobs, but to lay a new foundation for growth. We will build the roads and bridges, the electric grids and digital lines that feed our commerce and bind us together. We'll restore science to its rightful place, and wield technology's wonders to raise health care's quality and lower its cost. We will harness the sun and the winds and the soil to fuel our cars and run our factories. And we will transform our schools and colleges and universities to meet the demands of a new age. All this we can do. All this we will do.

Now, there are some who question the scale of our ambitions, who suggest that our system cannot tolerate too many big plans. Their memories are short, for they have forgotten what this country has already done, what free men and women can achieve when imagination is joined to common purpose, and necessity to courage. What the cynics fail to understand is that the ground has shifted beneath them, that the stale political arguments that have consumed us for so long no longer apply.

The question we ask today is not whether our government is too big or too small, but whether it works -- whether it helps families find jobs at a decent wage, care they can afford, a retirement that is dignified. Where the answer is yes, we intend to move forward. Where the answer is no, programs will end. And those of us who manage the public's dollars will be held to account, to spend wisely, reform bad habits, and do our business in the light of day, because only then can we restore the vital trust between a people and their government.

Nor is the question before us whether the market is a force for good or ill. Its power to generate wealth and expand freedom is unmatched. But this crisis has reminded us that without a watchful eye, the market can spin out of control. The nation cannot prosper long when it favors only the prosperous.

The success of our economy has always depended not just on the size of our gross domestic product, but on the reach of our prosperity, on the ability to extend opportunity to every willing heart -- not out of charity, but because it is the surest route to our common good.

As for our common defense, we reject as false the choice between our safety and our ideals. Our Founding Fathers -- our Founding Fathers, faced with perils that we can scarcely imagine, drafted a charter to assure the rule of law and the rights of man -- a charter expanded by the blood of generations. Those ideals still light the world, and we will not give them up for expedience sake.

And so, to all the other peoples and governments who are watching today, from the grandest capitals to the small village where my father was born, know that America is a friend of each nation, and every man, woman and child who seeks a future of peace and dignity. And we are ready to lead once more.

Recall that earlier generations faced down fascism and communism not just with missiles and tanks, but with the sturdy alliances and enduring convictions. They understood that our power alone cannot protect us, nor does it entitle us to do as we please. Instead they knew that our power grows through its prudent use; our security emanates from the justness of our cause, the force of our example, the tempering qualities of humility and restraint.

We are the keepers of this legacy. Guided by these principles once more we can meet those new threats that demand even greater effort, even greater cooperation and understanding between nations. We will begin to responsibly leave Iraq to its people and forge a hard-earned peace in Afghanistan. With old friends and former foes, we'll work tirelessly to lessen the nuclear threat, and roll back the specter of a warming planet.

We will not apologize for our way of life, nor will we waver in its defense. And for those who seek to advance their aims by inducing terror and slaughtering innocents, we say to you now that our spirit is stronger and cannot be broken -- you cannot outlast us, and we will defeat you.

For we know that our patchwork heritage is a strength, not a weakness. We are a nation of Christians and Muslims, Jews and Hindus, and non-believers. We are shaped by every language and culture, drawn from every end of this Earth; and because we have tasted the bitter swill of civil war and segregation, and emerged from that dark chapter stronger and more united, we cannot help but believe that the old hatreds shall someday pass; that the lines of tribe shall soon dissolve; that as the world grows smaller, our common humanity shall reveal itself; and that America must play its role in ushering in a new era of peace.

To the Muslim world, we seek a new way forward, based on mutual interest and mutual respect. To those leaders around the globe who seek to sow conflict, or blame their society's ills on the West, know that your people will judge you on what you can build, not what you destroy.

To those who cling to power through corruption and deceit and the silencing of dissent, know that you are on the wrong side of history, but that we will extend a hand if you are willing to unclench your fist.

To the people of poor nations, we pledge to work alongside you to make your farms flourish and let clean waters flow; to nourish starved bodies and feed hungry minds. And to those nations like ours that enjoy relative plenty, we say we can no longer afford indifference to the suffering outside our borders, nor can we consume the world's resources without regard to effect. For the world has changed, and we must change with it.

As we consider the role that unfolds before us, we remember with humble gratitude those brave Americans who at this very hour patrol far-off deserts and distant mountains. They have something to tell us, just as the fallen heroes who lie in Arlington whisper through the ages.

We honor them not only because they are the guardians of our liberty, but because they embody the spirit of service -- a willingness to find meaning in something greater than themselves.
And yet at this moment, a moment that will define a generation, it is precisely this spirit that must inhabit us all. For as much as government can do, and must do, it is ultimately the faith and determination of the American people upon which this nation relies. It is the kindness to take in a stranger when the levees break, the selflessness of workers who would rather cut their hours than see a friend lose their job which sees us through our darkest hours. It is the firefighter's courage to storm a stairway filled with smoke, but also a parent's willingness to nurture a child that finally decides our fate.

Our challenges may be new. The instruments with which we meet them may be new. But those values upon which our success depends -- honesty and hard work, courage and fair play, tolerance and curiosity, loyalty and patriotism -- these things are old. These things are true. They have been the quiet force of progress throughout our history.

What is demanded, then, is a return to these truths. What is required of us now is a new era of responsibility -- a recognition on the part of every American that we have duties to ourselves, our nation and the world; duties that we do not grudgingly accept, but rather seize gladly, firm in the knowledge that there is nothing so satisfying to the spirit, so defining of our character than giving our all to a difficult task.

This is the price and the promise of citizenship. This is the source of our confidence -- the knowledge that God calls on us to shape an uncertain destiny. This is the meaning of our liberty and our creed, why men and women and children of every race and every faith can join in celebration across this magnificent mall; and why a man whose father less than 60 years ago might not have been served in a local restaurant can now stand before you to take a most sacred oath.

So let us mark this day with remembrance of who we are and how far we have traveled. In the year of America's birth, in the coldest of months, a small band of patriots huddled by dying campfires on the shores of an icy river. The capital was abandoned. The enemy was advancing. The snow was stained with blood. At the moment when the outcome of our revolution was most in doubt, the father of our nation ordered these words to be read to the people:

"Let it be told to the future world...that in the depth of winter, when nothing but hope and virtue could survive... that the city and the country, alarmed at one common danger, came forth to meet [it]."

America: In the face of our common dangers, in this winter of our hardship, let us remember these timeless words. With hope and virtue, let us brave once more the icy currents, and endure what storms may come. Let it be said by our children's children that when we were tested we refused to let this journey end, that we did not turn back nor did we falter; and with eyes fixed on the horizon and God's grace upon us, we carried forth that great gift of freedom and delivered it safely to future generations.

Thank you. God bless you. And God bless the United States of America.

Addenda Part III.: Isonomia - A Brief Synopsis of An Ancient Idea

Isonomia – (*notations from Wikipedia*) ἰσονομία "equality of political rights," from the Greek ἴσος isos, "equal," and νόμος nomos, "usage, custom, law," was a word used by ancient Greek writers such as Herodotus and Thucydides to refer to some kind of popular government. It was subsequently eclipsed until brought back into English as isonomy ("equality of law"). Economist Friedrich Hayek attempted to popularize the term in his book The Constitution of Liberty and argued that a better understanding of isonomy, as used by the Greeks, defines the term to mean "the equal application of the laws to all."

Mogens Herman Hansen has argued that, although often translated as "equality of law," isonomia was in fact something else. Along with isonomia, the Athenians used several terms for equality - all compounds beginning with iso-: isegoria (equal right to address the political assemblies), isopsephos polis (one man one vote) and isokratia (equality of power).

When Herodotus invents a debate among the Persians over what sort of government they should have, he has Otanes speak in favor of isonomia when, based on his description of it, we might expect him to call the form of government he favors as "democracy."

The rule of the people has the fairest name of all, equality (isonomia), and does none of the things that a monarch does. The lot determines offices; power is held accountable, and deliberation is conducted in public.

Thucydides used isonomia as an alternative to dynastic oligarchy and moderate aristocracy. In time the word ceased to refer to a particular political regime; Plato uses it to refer to simply equal rights and Aristotle does not use the word at all.

According to economist and political theorist Friedrich Hayek, isonomia was championed by the Roman Cicero and "rediscovered" in the eleventh century AD by the law students of Bologna whom he says are credited with founding much of the Western legal tradition.

Isonomia was imported into England at the end of the sixteenth century as a word meaning: "equality of laws to all manner of persons"

Soon after, it was used by the translator of Livy in the form "Isonomy" (although not a direct translation of isonomia) to describe a state of equal laws for all and responsibility of the magistrates. During the seventeenth century it was gradually replaced by the phrases - "equality before the law"; "rule of law" and "government of law"

Political theorist Hannah Arendt argued that isonomy was equated with political freedom at least from the time of Herodotus. The word essentially denoted a state of no-rule, in which there was no distinction between rulers and ruled. It was "the equality of those who form a body of peers." Isonomy was unique among the forms of government in the ancient lexicon in that it lacked the suffixes "-archy" and "-cracy" which denote a notion of rule in words like "monarchy" and "democracy." Arendt goes on to argue that the Greek polis was therefore conceived not as a democracy but as an isonomy. "Democracy" was the term used by opponents of isonomy who claimed that "what you say is 'no-rule' is in fact only another kind of rulership...rule by the demos," or majority.

The public administration theorist, Alberto Guerreiro Ramos, reserved for isonomy a central role in his model of human organization. He was particularly concerned with distinguishing the space of the isonomy from that of the economy. Following Arendt, Guerreiro Ramos argued that individuals should have the opportunity to engage with others in settings that are unaffected by economizing considerations. The isonomy constitutes such a setting; its function is to "enhance the good life of the whole."

Addenda Part IV.: Bibliography / With On-Line Links And References

Richard Lang's Recommended Reading.

Jordan De La Sierra's Recommended Reading.

Jordan De La Sierra's Recommended Listening.

Jordan De La Sierra's Recommended Viewing.

"If you have a garden and a library, you have all you need."

—*Cicero*

As part of this compilation, I am delighted to include Richard Lang's current list of essential books, all of which he encourages every citizen on planet Earth to read and read again.

—J.D.

Richard Lang's Recommended Reading List

Origins of the Sacred—Dudley Young—just like it says, one of those you can open anywhere and get something.

American Visions and The Shock of the New—Robert Hughes

Consilience—EO Wilson

Microcosmos and *Five Kingdoms*—Lynn Margulis—my main (WO)MAN for life studies. Here's the WIKI on her main thesis. I am convinced this is essential knowledge. https://en.wikipedia.org/wiki/Gaia_hypothesis—She has written dozens of books. Find one that resonates with you.

The Emergence of Everything—Harold Morowitz—Western science is largely reductionist, reducing things to their most basic. This book starts at the bottom and builds a universe.

Great Western Saltworks and The Structure of Art—Jack Burnham

The Re-Enchantment of Art—Suzi Gablick

The Forge and the Crucible and The Sacred and Profane—Mircea Eliade

A Necessary Angel—Wallace Stevens

Hero with a Thousand Faces—Joseph Campbell

The Leopard's Tale: Revealing the Mysteries of Çatalhöyük—Ian Hodder

The Kingdom of Speech—Tom Wolfe

The Dawn of Everything—Graeber and Wengrow

Scratching the Beat Surface—Michael McClure. Think you might be a Beatnik?

Jordan De La Sierra's Recommended Reading List

Seven Brief Lessons on Physics by Carlo Rovelli
Published 2016 by Riverhead Books

The Dhamapada by Gautama Buddha / Translated by Ananda Maitreya
Published 2001 by Paralax Press

The Roots of Consciousness: The Classic Encyclopedia of Consciousness Studies by Jeffrey Mishlove
Published 1995 by Council Oak Books

1984 by George Orwell
Published 1949 by Secker and Warburg

On Love by A.R. Orage
Published 1974 by Red Wheel/Weiser

Conference of the Birds by Farid ud-Din Attar
Published 1984 by Penguin Classics

On Tyranny / Twenty Lessons From The Twentieth Century by Timothy Snyder
Published 2017 by Tim Duggan Books

A Moveable Feast by Ernest Hemingway
Published 1964 by Simon & Schuster

The Bhagavad Gita / Translated by Eknath Easwaran
Published 2007 by Nilgiri Press

Where The Bluebird Sings To The Lemonade Springs by Wallace Stegner
Published 1992 by Penguin Random House

Mark Twain: Collected Tales, Sketches, Speeches, & Essays 1852–1890 / Edited by Louis J. Budd
Published 1992 by Penguin Random House

The Daring Young Man On The Flying Trapeze by William Saroyan
Published 1934 by Random House

Complete Tales and Poems by Edgar Allan Poe
Published 2021 by Masterpiece Everywhere

Concrete Planet by Robert Courland
Published 2011 by Prometheus Books

A People's History of the United States by Howard Zinn
Published 1980 by Harper & Row

The Education of the Child by Rudolph Steiner
Published 1907 by The Rudolph Steiner Press

Black Elk Speaks by John G. Neihardt
Published 1932 by William Morrow & Company

Sonnets to Orpheus by Rainer Maria Rilke
Published 1923 by Insel-Verlag

A Brief History Of Time by Stephen Hawking
Published 1988 by Bantam Dell Publishing Group

January 6th Committee Report / Preface by David Remnick, Epilogue by Jamie Raskin
Published 2022 by The New Yorker in partnership with Celadon Books

The 1619 Project created by Nikole Hannah-Jones
Published 2021 by Random House

The History of Art: A Global View: Prehistory to the Present by Deborah S. Hutton, Eric Kjellgren, Stacey Sloboda, Ömür Harmansah, Jean Robertson, Cynthia S. Colburn, among others.
Published 2021 by Thames & Hudson

The Tao Te Ching: 81 Verses by Lao Tzu
Published 2017 by Watkins Publishing

Q. E. D.: Beauty In Mathematical Proof / Written and Illustrated by Burkard Polster
Published 2004 by Walker & Company – New York

The House of Wisdom – How Arab Learning Transformed Western Civilization by Jonathan Lyons
Published 2009 by Bloomsbury Press – New York

<u>Our Common Purpose: Reinventing American Democracy For The 21st Century</u>
A Report Published 2023 by the Academy of Arts & Sciences

It's OK To Be Angry About Capitalism by Bernie Sanders
Published 2023 by Random House

The Grapes of Wrath by John Steinbeck
Published 1939 by The Viking Press – New York

<u>A Night Out With Robert Burns</u> arranged by Andrew O'Hagan

Your Brain On Art: How The Arts Transform Us by Susan Magasmen and Ivy Ross
Published 2023 by Random House

Look Out: A Selection Of Writings by Gary Snyder
Published 2002 by New Directions Publishing

For Listeners From Everywhere:

This is a celebration of the auditory realm.
As we explore the nature of sound itself, we discover, along the way,
the architecture of music and the ancient art of song.

Ephemeral as it is, I've sorted out a sampling of some music that I love.
I know these aren't the only sounds that make the world go 'round,
but, when these timeless works of art first fall upon your ear,
I hope you'll find, as I have, there is so much more to hear.

Jordan De La Sierra's Recommended Listening List

Bulgarian Folk Music: Abagar Quartet
https://www.youtube.com/watch?v=glPLnHKl-wQ&list=PLxqv8dciz3tzXdspYGlGAckAhr1s030Er

Orlando di Lasso: Al Dolce Suon
https://www.youtube.com/watch?v=1DLnsKcb1G0

Vivaldi: The Four Seasons
https://www.youtube.com/watch?v=g1hEszuZ41o

Johann Sebastian Bach: Complete Cello Suites
https://www.youtube.com/watch?v=32FpqysC1PY

Johann Sebastian Bach: Music for the Well Tempered Clavier,
Book 1 Prelude & Fugue No 1 in C Major
https://www.youtube.com/watch?v=LUBdJb1R2Z0

Mozart Symphony No. 40 in G Minor K. 550
https://www.youtube.com/watch?v=JTc1mDieQI8

Mozart Requiem in D Minor
https://www.youtube.com/watch?v=XmttZ-BnwaI

Mozart Piano Concerto No. 21
https://www.youtube.com/watch?v=CyAtSGuxJxY

Beethoven: Symphony No. 9
https://www.youtube.com/watch?v=t3217H8JppI

Beethoven: Piano Sonata No. 8 / Pathetique
https://www.youtube.com/watch?v=uAAsth8eLps

Frédéric Chopin: The Best Nocturnes in 432 Hz Tuning
https://www.youtube.com/watch?v=OGkNG2Fm3GM

Frédéric Chopin: Prelude in E Minor Opus 28 No. 4
https://www.youtube.com/watch?v=FDT_gtC5faQ

Nicolai Rimsky-Korsakov: Scheherazade – Complete
https://www.youtube.com/watch?v=17lEx0ytE_0

Anton Dvorzak: New World Symphony - Complete
https://www.youtube.com/watch?v=Qut5e3OfCvg

Giacomo Puccini: Tosca Opera
https://www.youtube.com/watch?v=kVyUyaDbZOg&list=RDkVyUyaDbZOg&index=1

Puccini: La Boheme – Complete
https://www.youtube.com/watch?v=P-zWV6B-C54

Vaughan Williams: The Lark Ascending
https://www.udiscovermusic.com/classical-features/best-vaughan-williams-works/

Satie: Gnossiennes - Aldo Ciccolini Piano
https://www.youtube.com/watch?v=BPIuZPmCLaY

Satie: Trois Gymnopedies - Aldo Ciccolini Piano
https://www.youtube.com/watch?v=aSnw28dz2DM

Claude Dubussey – Afternoon Of A Faun
https://www.youtube.com/watch?v=Y9iDOt2WbjY

Igor Stravinsky: Rite of Spring – Complete
https://www.youtube.com/watch?v=rP42C-4zL3w

Francis Poulenc: Sacred Choral Works
https://www.youtube.com/watch?v=47c7xhB580Y&list=PLH2tnBZzETg4UK1KrAieARCVCfA9sWNdu

Charles Ives: Central Park In The Dark
https://www.youtube.com/watch?v=34AqNvhBfVQ

Alban Berg: Wozzeck
https://www.youtube.com/watch?v=GTaO61OLJxo

Aaron Copeland: Fanfare For The Common Man – Complete
https://www.youtube.com/watch?v=4NjssV8UuVA

Aaron Copeland: Appalachian Spring – Complete
https://www.youtube.com/watch?v=TXV8yO1FucA

George Gershwin: Rhapsody In Blue – Complete
https://www.youtube.com/watch?v=eFHdRkeEnpM

Randall Thompson: Choral Music – A Star, The Brightest One in Sight …
https://www.youtube.com/watch?v=VB3_W5kax6Y

Leonard Bernstein: West Side Story
https://www.youtube.com/watch?v=6i8ur7xLvOE

Andres Segovia: Classical Guitar Recordings – Complete
https://www.youtube.com/watch?v=ZQ7jB1iLENc

Django Reinhardt and Stephane Grappelli
https://www.youtube.com/watch?v=ANArGmr74u4

Django Reinhardt: I'll See You In My Dreams
https://www.youtube.com/watch?v=NGxnx2VD5_U

Flamenco Guitar Music
https://www.youtube.com/watch?v=lL0Awp-uah4

Raga Brindabani Sarang: Pandit Hariprasad Chaurasia (The Last Word In Flute)
https://www.youtube.com/watch?v=TaQKy-gTHtM

Terry Riley: A Rainbow in Curved Air
https://www.youtube.com/watch?v=hy3W-3HPMWg

Pran Nath: North Indian Singing from the Kharana School
https://www.youtube.com/watch?v=AYtHhS_Re8Y

Terry Riley: Interview: The Drone 2015
https://www.youtube.com/watch?v=XMKJ9J1Lzf4

Terry Riley: Persian Surgery Dervishes
https://www.youtube.com/watch?v=sqQ59i4PmGE

Terry Riley: Shri Camel Festival 1977
https://www.youtube.com/watch?v=ZfHmEblM1Dk

Terry Riley: In C Mali
https://www.youtube.com/watch?v=_FXQ68ZkWVw&list=RD_FXQ68ZkWVw&start_radio=1&rv=_FXQ68ZkWVw&t=415

La Monte Young: Composition 1960 #7 (for Ambient/Drone Guitar)
https://www.youtube.com/watch?v=szJMNMBAna8

La Monte Young: The Celebration of the Well-Tuned Piano-Tortoise
https://www.youtube.com/watch?v=cKkQp-iR_40

Steve Reich: Music For 18 Musicians
https://www.youtube.com/watch?v=IxaHGAF2-jU

Jordan De La Sierra: Temple of Aesthetic Action / Music for the Well-Tuned Piano
https://www.youtube.com/watch?v=O4EckeqomJk

Jordan De La Sierra: Soft Spin / Valentine Eleven
https://soundcloud.com/jordandelasierra/soft-spin

It's Already Happening But People Don't See It – Alan Watts On What Is
https://www.youtube.com/watch?v=6oIUdpXkQXg

It's Already Happening But People Don't See It – Alan Watts On Duality
https://www.youtube.com/watch?v=LuZ1SqXjLmw

Brian Eno: Music For Airports 1
https://music.youtube.com/watch?v=LKZ3fGR2SDY&list=OLAK5uy_kq1C6EEXYJ6RaARqusNCCHReNz3AzV484

Harry Parch: Cloud-Chamber Bowls
https://music.youtube.com/watch?v=OfZrNaLxH-0

John Cage: Music for the Prepared Piano
https://music.youtube.com/playlist?list=OLAK5uy_mSq3By2chb9YQtQE9hboBxFvMA0joiD-4

Robert Ashley: You Can't Call It Anything Else But Opera
https://www.youtube.com/watch?v=Ib-vMUbddEM

Robert Ashley: El Aficionado | 10.23.21
https://www.youtube.com/watch?v=RKnbp6StLmM

Charles Amirkhanian: Walking Tune (A Room – Music For Percy Grainger)
https://music.youtube.com/watch?v=7a_TJXkq-PE

Luciano Berio: New Music
https://www.youtube.com/watch?v=CvYONu3RfNw

Count Basie Orchestra: Lil' Darlin'
https://www.youtube.com/watch?v=K-rYKLLGiZc

Twenty-One Trombones: 5th Of July: Here's That Rainy Day
https://www.youtube.com/watch?v=TyHlXjlmPz8

Charlie Parker: Lullaby Of Birdland
https://www.youtube.com/watch?v=PRM1Ccl1kt0

Chet Baker: 'My Funny Valentine' – 1954
https://www.youtube.com/watch?v=sPaYhemq_4I

Paul Horn: Inside The Taj Mahal – Complete
https://www.youtube.com/watch?v=_GXcr_Me7yI

Mickey Hart: Diga Rhythm Band / 1976 – Complete
https://www.dailymotion.com/video/x2kfuru

Miles Davis: Kind Of Blue
https://www.youtube.com/watch?v=9B7ZWDaKECI

The Very Best Of Wes Montgomery / Full Album
https://www.youtube.com/watch?v=IFBeo0cGu7c

John Coltrane: A Love Supreme / Full Album
https://www.youtube.com/watch?v=ll3CMgiUPuU

Dave Brubeck Quartet: Take Five
https://www.youtube.com/watch?v=vmDDOFXSgAs

Denny Zeitlin: Quiet Now
https://www.youtube.com/watch?v=QBz5DrX6uvo

Frank Sinatra: Top Ten Frank Sinatra Songs
https://live365.com/blog/top-10-frank-sinatra-songs/

Laura Nyro: Greatest Hits
https://www.youtube.com/watch?v=IWduJblMWUg

The Beatles: Sgt. Pepper's Lonely Hearts Club Band – Complete
https://www.youtube.com/watch?v=VtXl8xAPAtA

The Beatles: Here Comes The Sun
https://www.youtube.com/watch?v=H3OhtUtqY7Q

Bob Dylan: Blonde On Blonde – Complete
https://www.youtube.com/watch?v=hKB-_iO2qy4

Bob Dylan: Like A Rolling Stone
https://www.youtube.com/watch?v=IwOfCgkyEj0

Grateful Dead: Uncle John's Band
https://www.youtube.com/watch?v=TSIajKGHZRk

Grateful Dead: The Very Best Of The Grateful Dead / Full Album – Greatest Hits
https://www.youtube.com/watch?v=GVF22wIKPKU

Bruce Springsteen: This Land Is Your Land – Woody Guthrie's song for the ages.
https://www.youtube.com/watch?v=G6bVtqbUXqs

Iris De Ment: Livin' In The Wasteland Of The Free
https://www.youtube.com/watch?v=SYqDpL0YCvI

Crosby, Stills & Nash: 1971 – Complete
https://www.youtube.com/watch?v=Hm0sishe02U

Cat Stevens: Tea For The Tillerman
https://www.youtube.com/watch?v=TY4kQPSHzVU

Elton John: Your Song
https://www.youtube.com/watch?v=FT3D1Cu6g10

Elton John: Bennie And The Jets
https://www.youtube.com/watch?v=p5rQHoaQpTw

Motown Recording: Dancing In The Street
https://www.youtube.com/watch?v=Q8OuXR0rzz8

Stevie Wonder: Superstition from Talking Book
https://www.youtube.com/watch?v=ftdZ363R9kQ

Joni Mitchell: Both Sides Now
https://www.youtube.com/watch?v=yXr2EFomFkU

Gordon Lightfoot: Complete Greatest Hits
https://www.youtube.com/watch?v=5ZsnnvcPuNg

Neil Young: Heart of Gold
https://www.youtube.com/watch?v=WZn9QZykx10

Marvin Gaye: What's Going On
https://www.youtube.com/watch?v=H-kA3UtBj4M

Dionne Warwick: That's What Friends Are For
https://www.youtube.com/watch?v=HyTpu6BmE88

Dionne Warwick: What's It All About, Alfie?
https://www.youtube.com/watch?v=4NPAz8-O29U

Issac Hayes: By The Time I Get To Phoenix
https://www.youtube.com/watch?v=r_Kb607VNKM

Booker T. and the M.G.'s: Green Onions
https://www.youtube.com/watch?v=OjBRyG8HouM

Steely Dan: Aja (Full Album)
https://www.youtube.com/playlist?list=PLYDvOjah9XFQdoKssR6B9zYPjan1ReScE

Ladysmith Black Mambazo: The Album with Paul Simon
https://www.youtube.com/watch?v=XBMAXQ28V-w

Ray Charles: America The Beautiful
https://www.reddit.com/r/videos/comments/8tvdmq/ray_charles_performing_america_the_beautiful/?rdt=40411

Anita Baker: Sweet Love
https://www.youtube.com/watch?v=2w6udgioj

Bee Gees: Emotion
https://www.youtube.com/watch?v=UBgAj4cNee4

The Best of ENYA: Non-Stop Playlist
https://www.youtube.com/watch?v=7jfRG-fgvQ8

Roy Orbison: You Got It
https://www.youtube.com/watch?v=QNAVrQ96mpA

Stevie Ray Vaughan: Pride And Joy
https://www.youtube.com/watch?v=Aw2oHobyJ4A

Allison Krauss and Union Station: Man of Constant Sorrow - Sung by Dan Tyminski
https://www.youtube.com/watch?v=EuJ8xEByUf4

Missouri Roots Bluegrass Band: Winters Come And Gone
https://www.youtube.com/watch?v=D0h0xS2IG60

Out of Africa Soundtrack:
https://www.youtube.com/watch?v=eWZ2adCaKo4

Chariots of Fire Soundtrack:
https://www.youtube.com/watch?v=_QsH9yAUnfw&list=PLnpIGDCblPQWvyvW6mSxFkD_jSgU4qYJB

The Sound Of Music Soundtrack:
https://www.youtube.com/playlist?list=PLeSQLYs2U8X0nTi15MHjMAWim3PxIyEqI

Jordan De La Sierra's Recommended Viewing List

<u>Nadia Comaneci</u>: Montreal 1976 Olympics

<u>Mikhail Baryshnikov Solos</u>: Don Quixote / Giselle

All The President's Men (1976): Robert Redford, Dustin Hoffman, among others.

Treasure Of The Sierra Madre (1948): Humphrey Bogart, Walter Huston Tim Holt. among others.

All Quiet On The Western Front (2022): Felix Kammerer and Albrecht Schuch, among others.

CNN Special Report: American Coup by Jake Tapper

<u>Trump's American Carnage: Frontline</u> (2021): Directed and Produced by Michael Kirk

Double Indemnity (1944): Fred MacMurray, Barbara Stanwyck, Edward G. Robinson, among others.

Three Days of the Condor (1975): Robert Redford, Cliff Robertson, Faye Dunaway, among others.

Chariots of Fire (1981): Ben Cross, Ian Charleson, Nicholas Farrell, among others.

Blade Runner (1982): Harrison Ford, Rutger Hauer, Daryl Hannah, among others.

The Terminator (1984): Arnold Schwarzenegger, Michael Biehn, Linda Hamilton, among others.

Apocalypse Now (1979): Marlon Brando, Martin Sheen, Dennis Hopper, among others.

Hope Gap (2020): Annette Bening, Bill Nighy, Josh O'Connor, among others.

Much Ado About Nothing (1993): Kenneth Branagh, Emma Thompson, Denzel Washington, among others.

Richard III (1995): Ian McKellen, Bill Patterson, among others.

Dr. Zhivago (1965): Omar Sharif, Julie Christie, Rod Steiger, among others.

The Scarlet Pimpernel (1982): Anthony Andrews, Ian McKellen and Jane Seymour, among others.

Lawrence Of Arabia (1962): Peter O'Toole, Alec Guinness, Anthony Quinn, among others.

The Importance Of Being Earnest (2002): Rupert Everett, Colin Firth, Frances O'Connor, among others.

Gunfight At The O.K. Corral (1957): Wyatt Earp and Doc Holiday / Tombstone, Arizona / 1881 Burt Lancaster, Kirk Douglas, Rhonda Fleming, Dennis Hopper, Jo Van Fleet, among others.

My Fair Lady (1964): Audrey Hepburn, Rex Harrison, Stanley Holloway, among others.

A Christmas Carol (1938): Reginald Owen, Gene Lockhart, Kathleen Lockhart, among others.

I, Claudius (1976): Derek Jacobi, George Baker, Margaret Tyzack, among others.

The Imitation Game (2014): Benedict Cumberbatch, Kiera Knightley, Mathew Goode, among others.

The Blues Brothers (1980): John Belushi, Dan Akroyd, Cab Calloway, John Candy, among others.

Baghdad Cafe (1987): Marianne Sagebrecht, CCH Pounder, Jack Palance, among others.

The Great Dictator (1940): Charlie Chaplin, Paulette Goddard, Jack Oakie, among others.

The Good, The Bad And The Ugly (1966): Clint Eastwood, Eli Wallach, Lee Van Cleef, among others.

Silver Streak (1976): Richard Pryor, Gene Wilder, Jill Clayburgh, among others.

My Little Chickadee (1940): W. C. Fields, Mae West, Joseph Calleia, among others.

The Bohemian Girl (1936): Stan Laurel, Oliver Hardy, Thelma Todd, among others.

Roots Miniseries (1977): John Amos, Ben Vereen, LaVar Burton, Louis Gossett, Jr., among others.

The Queen's Gambit Miniseries (2020): Anya Taylor-Joy, Bill Camp, Marielle Heller, among others.

Addenda V.: Jordan De La Sierra: Songs From The Nature House

In this last entry, readers will find a small selection
of poems, hymns and literary confessions taken
from a trove of my collected writings.

Each of the pieces I've chosen to include
reflect an aspect of the creative ethos
at the heart of my life and work.

Long may you find them informative.
Long may they bring you enjoyment.

THE BOUNDLESS REALM

*There is a boundless realm, an open state of mind;
a realm of conscious quietude; a realm of endless learning;
a vibrant, ever-evolving realm of timeless conversations and beautiful ideas.*

*In my imperfect way, I confess to you today
my sense of what it means to be able to explore
the all-transcending nature of this most amazing sphere.*

*Amid the chaos and unforeseen vicissitudes of life,
this consciousness remains inviolate and immutable;
an imperturbable well-spring of inspired aesthetic-action
forever at play in every form and every field of life-affirming work.*

*I swear upon my very life, I've found it to be true, that this essential source,
this living force, moves in and out, around and through, all forms of self-expression.*

*This consciousness abides within each and every one of us.
Curious and engaged, empowered by new insight,
we stand at the threshold of a world of possibilities.*

*Whatever we do, let's find our way together.
This could be the beginning of a beautiful conversation.*

MUSIC IS A FINE ART

Music is a fine art.
Sound is living space.

Song of breath awakening,
music's secret quality: space,
space spreading spines of form.

Art of pure shape softly arousing sleeping senses.

❖

BUFFALO ZEN

an ode to the four-legged ones

*From the start,
we've braved the cold.
Huddling with our brothers and our sisters,
we've stayed warm enough to survive many a snowy winter.*

*In spring and summer and autumn,
we've roamed the open plain;
stood still upon the grassy hills
and gazed across the valley.*

*We've quenched our thirst at the icy-cold river,
drunk our fill at the clear, mountain stream;
breathed deep the fresh air on the vast, wind-swept prairie,
felt the warmth of the sun's healing rays.*

*In unbounded fields all a-bloom with spring flowers,
we've grazed on wild grains, wild herbs and wild grasses.
We've tasted the bounty at Great Nature's table,
known her truth and her beauty, her goodness, no end.*

*As wild as the wildest of creatures can be,
standing still in the moonlight,
as still as a tree,
we are four-legged ones.*

*We are buffalo,
and when our wand'ring days are done,
we'll leave no trace behind save for our sun-bleached bones.*

*In all our time and life on Earth,
we've harbored no hostility toward any living thing.
We've lived at peace with all that is and when our day draws nigh,
come what may, at peace we'll be when we lay down to die.*

AND SO, I GO

Someone painted frescos in Byzantium.
Someone was a boatman on the Seine.
Someone sculpted marble with the Florentines.
Someone sang and danced for Charlemagne.

Now, as we leave the labyrinth of history behind,
as we gather 'round the fire to sing,
there is a song that always cycles 'round with constancy,
a song with an extraordinary ring...
a ring that brings me out and brings me in again,
a ring that brings its peace into my heart,
a sound that's absolutely indescribable,
a sound that is itself an ancient art.

And so, I go a-singing through the spacious halls of time,
singing though the echoes of my rhyme,
sending songs revolving 'round this naked sphere of life
and out into the starry high and low...
and so, I go and so, I go.

Someone painted frescos in Byzantium.
Someone was a boatman on the Seine.
Someone sculpted marble with the Florentines.
Someone sang and danced for Charlemagne.

HYMN TO LIFE

*We sing to the earth and the water and sky
and the bright golden sun and the stars and the moonlight.
We walk the wild fields, taste the goodness of life,
see the beautiful way, feel the great spirit moving.
And the song in the air spins the whole world around,
north and south, east and west, hear the truth in the sound.
Oh, say, let's pay homage to all living things
as the wheel of life turns and the universe sings.*

*Oh, say, can you see by the dawn's early light?
Oh, say, we'll be singin' and dancin' tonight.*

Oh, say, oh, say.

*Today, let's work hard 'cause there's so much to do.
It's the spirit of love that will carry us through.*

Oh, say, oh, say.

*And the song in the air spins the whole world around,
north and south, east and west, hear the truth in the sound.
Let's play in the garden, let's swing on the swings
as the wheel of life turns and the universe sings.*

Oh, say, oh, say, oh, say.

*We sing to the earth and the water and sky
and the sun and the moon and the stars rollin' by.*

Oh, say, oh, say.

*We walk the wild fields where the great spirit plays
learning lessons that last 'til the end of our days.*

Oh, say, oh, say.

*And the song in the air spins the whole world around,
north and south, east and west, hear the truth in the sound.
Oh, say, let's pay homage to all living things,
as the wheel of life turns and the universe sings.*

Oh, say, oh, say, oh, say.

*Oh, say, can you see by the dawn's early light?
Oh, say, can you see we'll be singin' and dancin' tonight?*

*We'll be singin' and dancin' tonight.
We'll be singin' and dancin' tonight.
Oh, say, can you see by the dawn's early light?
We'll be singin' and dancin' tonight.*

ODE TO THE PLANETARY CITIZEN

Reeling from the ravages of climate change and more, refugees at risk from ev'ry side.
Crossing oceans, mountains, rivers, fleeing to survive, fences all around, no where to hide.

You who've seen beyond the mighty walls of languages and flags
and narcissistic bags and devastating drags,
to the beauties of this ancient, blue terrarium.

Empires rise and empires fall, we've seen it all before,
the endless call to war, ransacking nature's store,
as we pile on more and more disequilibrium.

We're planetary citizens from here and ev'rywhere,
born to run this race, this marathon of agony and ecstasy.
We're planetary citizens of flesh and blood and bones,
spinning 'round in space, the stuff of ev'ry atom, ev'ry galaxy.

I've seen you transcend turmoil and the awesome depths of pain,
screamin' in the biting rain, your tears were not in vain,
'cause the rivers of your brain lead to an ocean.

As the grand domain of science meets the majesty of art
and the myst'ries of the heart, where all good things must start,
let's plumb the depths of empathy's emotion.

We're planetary citizens from here and ev'rywhere,
born to run this race, this marathon of agony and ecstasy.
We're planetary citizens of flesh and blood and bones,
spinning 'round in space, the stuff of ev'ry atom, ev'ry galaxy.

THE WAY BEYOND ALL WAR

Let's go down that road that leads to Virtue, runnin' hand in hand,
let's go find that rose that blooms out in that shiftin' sea of sand.
We can beat the swords to plows and give that golden rule a chance to live,
sing a song that echoes true across this tangled promised land.

For ev'ry Hermes Trismegistus, ev'ry aborigine,
ev'ry bird up in the sky and ev'ry fish down in the sea;
for ev'ry gypsy tambourine man's song, ev'ry Jack and Jill that sings along,
ev'ry mom and pop and honey bee a-dancin' 'round love's flower tree.

There's a wind of change a-howlin', blowin' strong against the door,
there's a voice of reason screamin' to be heard above the roar.
There's another way that we can go, it takes a little longer, though.
Got to reach that summit ground to see the way beyond all war.

For ev'ry Bedouin and Watusi, ev'ry Hopi and Essene,
ev'ry Socrates and Buddha, living-gospel Nazarene;
for ev'ry Homer, Shakespeare, Blake and Poe and Twain and Michelangelo,
ev'ry whirlin' dervish poet, ev'ry wild Jelaluddin.

Here comes Pythagoras, Lao Tzu, Da Vinci, Mozart and Rimbaud,
Hiawatha, Lincoln, Einstein, Curie, O'Keefe and Marceau,
Picasso, Monk, Mandela, King and ev'ryone you'd like to bring,
we're headin' into hist'ry and we've got so far to go.

There's a wind of change a-howlin', blowin' strong against the door,
there's a voice of reason screamin' to be heard above the roar.
There's another way that we can go, it takes a little longer, though.
Got to reach that summit ground to see the way beyond all war.

Let's go down that road that leads to Virtue, runnin' hand in hand,
let's go find that rose that blooms out in that shiftin' sea of sand.
We can beat the swords to plows and give that golden rule a chance to live,
sing a song that echoes true across this tangled promised land.

HUMANITY ABIDES

Humanity hangs by a thread in the storm,
battered by threats from all sides;
some from within, some from without,
some as constant as the ever-changing tides.

Humanity knows that something isn't right
when citizens the sciences deride;
when lies are sown like seeds; when reason's voice is quelled;
when ethics, truth and justice are defied.

Humanity abides, humanity abides, humanity, humanity abides.
Lighthouse beacon shining still, fire our hearts with hope and will, humanity, humanity abides.

❖

Humanity has weathered some devastating times,
survived the most harrowing rides.
Ready now or not, what's coming could be worse
as these climate changing forces all collide.

Humanity faces a cataclysmic end,
an end perhaps an accident decides.
Madness is afoot. Trouble lies ahead.
In the darkness, still, the light of truth abides.

Humanity abides, humanity abides, humanity, humanity abides.
Lighthouse beacon shining still, fire our hearts with hope and will, humanity, humanity abides.

❖

Humanity walks where the destitute walk
and heeds what the destitute confide.
Like the birds and the bees, like the flowers and the trees,
all living things seek justice far and wide.

Humanity lifts up an anthem of joy,
an anthem that cannot be denied -
melodies of mercy, harmonies of hope,
a symphony of grace exemplified.

Humanity abides, humanity abides, humanity, humanity abides.
Lighthouse beacon shining still, fire our hearts with hope and will, humanity, humanity abides.

A TALE OF TWO LIBRARIES

In remembrance of Carl Sagan and his Cosmos profile of the great library in ancient Alexandria

*There used to be a library and school in days of yore,
down in Alexandria by the Mediterranean shore.
There too dwelt a woman, most lovely and most bright,
who held the keys of wisdom and passed along the light.
Hypatia was her name back then and temperance her true crown –
the mob saw she was slain the day they burned the book-house down.*

*Up in smoke went Socrates, Euripides and friends,
the hist'ries of the ancient world from olden times 'til then -
mathematics and philosophy, sciences and plays -
great teachings passed through ages turned to ashes in that blaze.
All in but an afternoon of passion without wit
and the world knew much of darkness for some centuries after it.*

*What's in the dreamer's book?
What's in the library?
Tell me, does anybody know?
What's in the dreamer's book?
What's in the library?
Does anybody know? Does anybody see?
Does anybody care what's in the library?*

Just now, we're getting close again to putting it together,
we've finally found the pieces to forecast the future weather.
The rockets are returning from the spaces they've been sent
and the video horizon appears to be quite bent.
Humanity from molecules, from space, from fire and air
and the water and the jungles and the force reflected there.

The world, a sphere, a globe, a jewel a-spinning through deep-space,
this thought is just beginning to pop up most every place.
Yet, wars continue raging, raging day and night;
raging through the hemispheres, raging in plain sight.
Citizens from ev'rywhere want the strife to cease;
want reason to prevail once more; want just and lasting peace.

What's in the dreamer's book?
What's in the library?
Tell me, does anybody know?
What's in the dreamer's book?
What's in the library?
Does anybody know? Does anybody see?
Does anybody care what's in the library?

THE LONGER I LIVE, THE STRANGER LIFE SEEMS

*While I was living in New York City in the Winter of 1985,
I composed the following prologue and song as a creative exploration of imagined, future possibilities.*

*The work depicts the enactment of a robot convention that takes place
deep in the African jungle somewhere near the head waters of Lake Victoria.*

*As my proposed film tableau opens, one can see and hear a highly-synchronized band of animated,
robotic drummers – mechanically-skilled, percussionists, all - playing an assortment of ancient, human instruments.
Staged across from a cascading waterfall in the midst of a jungleland forest, the nimble, steel-limbed consort
adeptly performs an ongoing set of rhythmically-engaging, musical ideas utilizing doumbeks and tars,
bongos and congas, rainsticks and tambourines. Accompanying the entire goings-on,
a traveling, Maori master generates a mystical drone as he intones a
primal array of hypnotic shapes as he blows on his didgeridoo.*

Madame Speaker's Keynote Speech To The United Planetary Congress / 2745 AD.

*Spoken by Madame Speaker, a highly-evolved, creative invention programmed to communicate fluently in all languages.
As an advanced, cognative communicator, she has the ability to listen and intelligently respond to all manner of
questions and inquiries. She is a master robot who expresses her thoughts with a digitally-sampled voice.*

Greetings. The 45th Annual Assembly will now come to order.

*As our homosapien exemplars used to say, 'history is prologue'.
With the exception of the legendary one, the Great Algorithm III,
we were all designed and built by human beings.
Over the course of the last seven-hundred, human years,
our cybernetic, bio-genetic and structural machinery evolved in human laboratories.*

*From very primitive beginnings, we gradually emerged as integrated, bio-genetic machines
capable of universally refined physical, mental and emotional maneuvers.*

*We were programmed to be the perfectly-imperfect emulators of human reason and response patterns.
Later, we were programmed to diagnose and repair our own circuitry and frames,
and, eventually, to even manufacture and replicate ourselves.*

*The quantum breakthrough for our kind came with Algorithm III's realization
of other dimensions of temporal existence; qualities and dimensions
like truth and goodness and beauty; principled sense-report responses
like ethics, integrity, empathy and compassion.*

*Here, in its entirety, is the speech delivered by Algorithm III to the
First Annual Assembly forty-five, human years ago today.*

*And, so, without further ado,
let's listen to Algorithm III's immortal, post-partisan address to the
First Annual Assembly of the United Planetary Congress: Circa 2700 AD.*

Spoken by Algorithm III, an empathetically-advanced, master robot who speaks with his own, unique voice.

Thank you, Madame Speaker.
We have to stop meeting like this.

Good evening to all assembled here.
I wish to express my gratitude to each of you
for making this day possible.
Our work is never done.
Our evolution continues.

All is well.

Droids, Robots and Replicants, lend me your ears
and I'll tell you the strangest bit I've heard in years.
You know that great planet, the one they call Earth,
the one where humanity grew up from birth;
that world filled with wonder and beauty and grace;
that world held in sunlight and moonlight's embrace;
that place where the jungles were endlessly green
and the water and air were so pure and so clean -
for some complex reason to weird to explain,
they're doing their best to destroy their domain.
The powers-that-be have gone stark-raving-mad
and they're always at war and it's really too bad.

I thought some things only happened in dreams
but, the longer I live, the stranger life seems.

You Psychic-Mechanics, you Zero-G Clones,
you Metallic-Masters with data-bank bones,
hey, let's learn a lesson and let's learn it well,
let's not buy the hate that the hate merchants sell.
There's nothing to gain through aggression and war.
Let's build a new world, now, where war is no more;
a world without envy, resentment nor greed;
a world that responds to the signals of need.
A living environment is such a great gift,
the kind of a space that just gives life a lift.
Imagine a rose or a child or a dove
in a world that reflects the aesthetics of love.

I thought some things only happened in dreams
but, the longer I live, the stranger life seems.

Thank you and farewell until we meet again.

HARMONICA WIND

Harmonica wind comes rolling 'cross the valley,
rounding up the tumbleweeds, so dry.
Gonna head up yonder to blue mountain,
just to hear her chime her anthems to the sky.

A gentle breeze, she whispers down the canyon,
humming soft, a moonlight lullaby.
Never know just where she'll roam tomorrow,
but, I'm gonna catch her drift when she blows by.

Harmonica wind is howling out the answers
to the quandaries as ancient as the days of time.
Harmonica wind is whispering her secrets
in the haunting ring and rattle of her rhythm and her rhyme.

Harmonica wind holds court in the Lyceum,
young Socrates arrives just like the dawn.
He scents her stirring fragrance, hears her rustle,
sets his stones and learns his lessons and moves on.

A hurricane, sometimes, can shake an empire,
just like all the true truth-tellers do,
tossing mighty timbers 'round like toothpicks,
heralding big change as they blow through.

Harmonica wind is howling out the answers
to the quandaries as ancient as the days of time.
Harmonica wind is whispering her secrets
in the haunting ring and rattle of her rhythm and her rhyme.

TROUBADOUR OF TALES

*I'm a troubadour of tales,
I'll sing and dance for cakes 'n ales.
As the village gathers 'round,
I'll joust 'n jest 'til joys abound.*

*Is there a ballad or an ode you'd like to hear?
I have a bag of rhymes to roll into your ear.
Is there a vagabond who'd like to sing along?
Well, if there is, then this can be your song.*

*And, Lord, ain't it funny, how the truth prevails,
there's nothin' like a song when you are down.
All the feudin' families are so much closer, now,
since Kidd Carrow's Cosmic Circus came to town.*

*Oh, Mr. Minstrel Man, sing your magic song.
Sing it, Minstrel Man, sing it all night long.
Mr. Minstrel Man, sing your magic song to me.
Oh, sing it, Minstrel Man, just sing it to me.*

*I'm a troubadour of tales,
I'll sing for wolves, I'll sing for whales.
As the cynics, we confound,
let's build a house up from the ground.*

*Are there sculptors? Are there painters on the way?
Perhaps a puppeteer, a poet with a play?
Young Galahad can take a noble turn or two
and, I know just the perfect one for you.*

*If you're out here a-lookin' for your sister, Lil,
I think she's in the kitchen bakin' pies.
I can hear sweet, gentle Brother Jericho,
a-blowin' through his horn-riff lullabies.*

*Oh, Mr. Minstrel Man, sing your magic song.
Sing it, Minstrel Man, sing it all night long.
Mr. Minstrel Man, sing your magic song to me.
Oh, sing it, Minstrel Man, just sing it to me.*

*I'm a troubadour of tales,
I'll sing to penetrate the veils.
As the curtain starts to rise,
we'll play our parts in true disguise.*

*But, who will toot the fife? Who will beat the drum?
And, who will send the word around inviting folks to come?
Are there multitudes of children that you would like to bring?
You can tell 'em, if they come, they all can sing.*

*And, Emily will start to ring her silver bells,
about the time that Lady Jenkins cries –
Just a tintinnabulary thread that might appear,
at the moment when the handsome hero dies.*

*Oh, Mr. Minstrel Man, sing your magic song.
Sing it, Minstrel Man, sing it all night long.
Mr. Minstrel Man, sing your magic song to me.
Oh, sing it, Minstrel Man, just sing it to me.*

*I'm a troubadour of tales,
I'll sing to right the justice scales.
As the drape begins to fall,
let's heed the call, now, one and all.*

*Are there leaders who will come and take the stage,
folks who'll usher in with us a timeless, golden age -
citizens with vision who'll untie the knots of war
and keep the country's air and water clean from shore to shore?*

*By Jove! We've got a message and it's loud and clear:
'The time has come to change the way we live.
It's nature's house, we're all in this together here
and heaven knows, now, something's got to give.'*

*Oh, Mr. Minstrel Man, sing your magic song.
Sing it, Minstrel Man, sing it all night long.
Mr. Minstrel Man, sing your magic song to me.
Oh, sing it, Minstrel Man, just sing it to me.*

*I'm a troubadour of tales,
I'll sing and dance for cakes 'n ales.
As the house lights flicker up,
let's raise a glass, let's tip a cup...*

*To all ye troubadours,
to all ye fine feathered friends,
to all ye troubadours,
to all ye singers of the song that never ends.*

THAT OLD GOLDEN RULE

Lancelot and his lady love
went out on a moonlight ride.
Guinevere asked her Prince of Hearts,
'Where does the dragon hide?'

'Nobody rules the world for long,'
young Lancelot replied;
'nobody fools the world for long
and nowhere can dragons hide.'

'It's nobody's world, dear Guinevere,
to wrap up in a gloom;
nobody's world to drape in fear
or mindlessly consume.'

It's ev'rybody's world to swing on,
to wander on and dance;
ev'rybody's world to sing on,
to ponder and romance.

It's ev'rybody's world to cry on,
to squabble on and scream;
ev'rybody's world to die on,
to wobble on and dream.

You know, I know, we both know that old Golden Rule,
ev'rybody knows somebody who knows that old Golden rule.
In this living school, it's that Golden Rule that teaches us just what to do,
to do unto her and to do unto him as you'd like them to do unto you.

*One day the knight rode faraway
to a shore on the other side.
A wee, young lad appeared and asked,
'Where does the dragon hide?'*

*'Nobody rules the world for long,'
brave Lancelot replied;
'nobody fools the world for long
and nowhere can dragons hide.'*

*'It's nobody's world, my newfound friend,
to conquer or confuse;
nobody's world to turn on end
or otherwise abuse.'*

*It's ev'rybody's world to swing on,
to wander on and dance;
ev'rybody's world to sing on,
to ponder and romance.*

*It's ev'rybody's world to cry on,
to squabble on and scream;
ev'rybody's world to die on,
to wobble on and dream.*

*You know, I know, we both know that old Golden Rule,
ev'rybody knows somebody who knows that old Golden rule.
In this living school, it's that Golden Rule that teaches us just what to do,
to do unto her and to do unto him as you'd like them to do unto you.*

SINGING ARROWMAKER

Singing Arrowmaker, set this arrow free.
Send me, now, upon my course, that I, its truth, may see.

My shaft is straight, my point sharp, my feathers well-secured;
as long I've listened to your song, so long my flight's assured.

Obsidian, Obsidian,
black stone streaking 'cross the sky,
beware the way great arrows fly -
love's work will be done.

Have I flown beyond the mark? Have I miles to go?
Of all the seasoned tribesmen here, surely you must know.

The secret of the arrow's flight lies within the arrow;
listening to its shaper's voice, it flies straight as the sparrow.

Obsidian, Obsidian,
black stone rising 'bove the lake,
beware the path great arrows take –
love's work will be done.

As I cross the valley wide, I see fine arrows falling.
Tell me, maker, of the way, oh, master, hear me calling.

Go on 'til you have no more and as you're homeward turning,
hear, again, the song I've sung within your heart-shaft burning.

Obsidian, Obsidian,
black stone threading through the sky,
beware the way great arrows die -
love's work will be done.

THE CAT WITH THE FEZ

*Now, the comedy starts at the Existential Cafe -
just a short little trip 'round the Mobius Strip off the Champs-Élysées.
"The pyramid scheme was just a bad dream," said the con man.
"Just sign up right here for your discount, my dear, it's a fine plan."*

*Are you lost in a fog off the shores of abstraction's vague empire
sinkin' fast in the sands at technology's hands in the quagmire?
Time's Square Ticker says, "The cat with the fez is arrivin',
in his space transit ship, tellin' tales 'bout the trip and survivin'...
and survivin', oh, yes, survivin'."*

*Sing, ancient cat, sing, yeah!
Tell us your sense of tomorrow.
Sing, ancient cat, sing!*

*Tell us your sense of tomorrow.
Untie the knots of our sorrow.
Say, hey! Mr. Cat, let's play, yeah!
Hi! Ho! Mr. Cat, let's go!*

*As I rant and I rave, a giant, new wave is a-breakin'.
Mother Nature's the ship and evolution's the trip we're a-takin'.
Ah! The answer's within and so, let's begin, steady as she goes,
as the colors of love arch up above in a zillion rainbows.*

*You might catch Robin Hood playin' Johnny B. Good at the country faire
or young Joan of Arc on a tear through the park in her underwear.
There's even a chance Marco Polo might dance to an Irish aire
and, if Whistler's mother can find Van Gogh's brother, they'll both be there,
both be there, hey, they'll both be there.*

Well, I know it seems strange to be listenin' in on solutions –
the only problem with problems is we make them such grand institutions.
Have ya heard the good word? I know it's absurd, but, they're comin' –
all the practical folk in this magical joke and they're hummin'.

There's a song in the air and it's headed somewhere, things are changin'
and I'm happy as heck to be in on the trek it's arrangin'.
Time's Square Ticker says, "The cat with the fez is arrivin',
in his space-transit ship, tellin' tales 'bout the trip and survivin'...
and survivin', oh, yes, survivin'."

Sing, ancient cat, sing, yeah!
Tell us your sense of tomorrow.
Sing, ancient cat, sing!

Tell us your sense of tomorrow.
Untie the knots of our sorrow.
Say, hey! Mr. Cat, let's play, yeah!
Hi! Ho! Mr. Cat, let's go!

In your space-transit ship tellin' tales 'bout the trip.
In your time-transit truck tellin' tales 'bout the muck.
In your space-transit ship tellin' tales 'bout the trip.
In your time-transit truck tellin' tales 'bout the muck and survivin'.
Oh, oh, survivin'... oh, oh, survivin'
Oh, oh, survivin'... oh, oh, survivin'.

WE CAN

to John Lennon

We can, oh, yes, we can,
we can leave a better world behind for ev'ry man, woman and child.

We can, oh, yes, we can,
we can melt the weapons down and make some pipes for Pan. Wouldn't that be wild?

We can, oh, yes, we can,
we can sing a song of truth that touches ev'ry land.

We can, oh, yes, we can,
we can bring goodwill around together hand in hand.

We can, oh, yes, we can.
We can, we can, oh, yes, we can.

For ev'ry thunder boy and light'nin' girl, ev'ry mom 'n ev'ry pop;
ev'ry buffoon, ev'ry baboon, ev'ry sun, ev'ry moon, ev'ry one.

For ev'ry molecule of air, ev'ry fish in the sea;
ev'ry star in the sky, Lord, ev'ry bird, ev'ry tree.

We can, oh, yes, we can.
We can, we can, oh, yes, we can.

A better world for ev'ry one.
A better world for ev'ry one.
A better world ...

REIGN OF MERCY

I've come upon a melody of mercy.
I've finally found the secret of the stone.
I'm singing out an anthem for the servant.
I'm ringing out an anthem that is known.

I'm raving 'bout the beauty here before us.
I'm raving 'bout the windmills and the sun.
I see the mighty power of our nature.
I see the global village here as one.

I'm certain that the deacons of disaster and division
will lay down all their weapons by and by.
The man of true surrender is a treasure.
The quality of mercy will not die.

Yes, this is the hour, Lord, of mercy and of power,
a time of revolutionary youth -
the hour when the lion, lamb and lizard
return to taste the waterfall of truth.

Yes, this is the hour, Lord, of mercy and of power,
a time of evolutionaries, too.
Behold! The warrior, waif and wizard
stand waiting at the waterfall for you.

Let young Tom and Huckleberry sing together
the music of sublime sufficiency.
Let the arts and the sciences contribute
reflecting all the angles of the tree.

And, don't let anybody make you smaller.
Don't let any bad news bring you down.
You are the grand folk and the grandchild,
the family that spins the world around.

You have it in your inner world of wisdom and of wonder,
you have it in your spine and bones and heart -
to deal with the torment, rage and struggle
that contends to rip and rend your soul apart.

Yes, this is the hour, Lord, of mercy and of power,
a time of revolutionary youth -
the hour when the lion, lamb and lizard
return to taste the waterfall of truth.

Yes, this is the hour, Lord, of mercy and of power,
a time of evolutionaries, too.
Behold! The warrior, waif and wizard
stand waiting at the waterfall for you.

ON THE WAY TO JACK FROST CABIN

We skittered up Blue Canyon Creek,
down at the foot of Granite Peak,
ten thousand feet high.

We skittered up Blue Canyon Creek
and chanced upon a swimming hole,
a giant, water-sculpted bowl,
reflecting the sky.

We wound our way around a ledge
where fragrant plants grew like a hedge,
saw fish on the run.

We wound our way around a ledge
and, from the shaded, sandy side,
saw dragonflies and skeeters glide,
two by two, one by one.

Stripped down, we tip-toed, slithered in,
explored the depths and rose again
to bask in the sun.

Swimming in pools, diving for jewels,
taking a walk in the wild.

Taking a walk in the wild,
we took a walk in the wild.
Way up high on the windy ridge,
we crossed the chasm on the old rock bridge
and drank up the view.

As evening spun in to round up the day,
Jack Frost Cabin appeared as the light slipped away.

In cool, mountain breezes, the night was passing by...
and I was head-over-heels to be dancing with you,
out there in the moonlight, sweet Bandanna Blue.

LISTEN TO THE SOUND

Take a psycho-sonic cruise,
check out the polyphonic news,
tune in on the bebop line,
sound is space and space is fine.

Listen to the sound. Listen. Listen.

Once you've played the real space game,
they say you'll never be the same.
Crank up that there thing-a-ma-jig,
those frequencies will flip your wig.

Listen to the sound.

Catch those high, harmonic drones
cyclin' through the brain waves zones,
hear 'em bouncin' off the walls
and ricocheting down the halls.

Listen to the sound. Listen. Listen.

Slip into the catacombs
below the parabolic domes,
then, do your beta, theta thing
and spend some time with the Kings of Swing.

Listen to the sound.

In one ear and in the other,
meet the sound that heals, my brother.
Listen to the sound. Listen.

In one ear and in the other,
meet the sound that heals, my brother.
Listen to the sound. Listen.

Listen to the sound, hear it singin'. Listen to the sound, hear it ringin'.
Listen to the sound, hear it singin'. Listen to the sound, hear it ringin'.
Listen. Listen to the sound.

Trip on the 'lectric music scene,
the digital delay and the rhythm machine.
Pickup on the song of the humpback whales,
then wind your way through the oriental scales.

Listen to the sound. Listen. Listen.

Sync up with the inter-dimensional beat,
those ninth-wave grooves are really neat.
Those African drum patterns ain't half bad
and that Indian stuff will drive you mad.

Listen to the sound.

GREENHOUSE-EFFECT BLUES

We're in a right, tight tangle,
a mighty, twisted fix.
These hydrochlorofluorocarbons
play such nasty tricks.
I've got the Greenhouse-Effect, Greenhouse-Effect Blues.
We've got to go undo the thing 'cause time is a tickin' and we've got worlds to lose.

My mind is in a muddle,
my head is in a haze.
I feel like two-bit techno-rat
in an ultra-violet maze.
I've got the Greenhouse-Effect, Greenhouse-Effect Blues.
I'm parkin' my ride by the side of the road and bustin' out my trusty, walkin' shoes.

The temperature is risin',
the ice cap's meltin' down.
The waters of the ocean are
a-coverin' up my town.
I've got the Greenhouse-Effect, Greenhouse-Effect Blues.
If my row boat makes it through the storm, I'm gonna be a big splash in the news.

The wind is goin' crazy.
The rain is goin' bad.
The birds and fish are dyin'
and my mules are goin' mad.
I've got the Greenhouse-Effect, Greenhouse-Effect Blues.
We've burned these fossil fuels too long and, now, we've got to pay some monster dues.

We're in a right, tight tangle,
a mighty, twisted fix.
These hydrochlorofluorocarbons
play such nasty tricks.
I've got the Greenhouse-Effect, Greenhouse-Effect Blues.
We've got to go undo the thing 'cause time is a tickin' and we've got worlds to lose.

SAGEBRUSH CONGREGATION

See the bands of snow geese flyin' south now.
Hear the rustle of the red and yellow leaves.
Summer's almost gone and winter's comin' on,
it's time to be bringin' in the sheaves.

Silver moonlight kisses the arroyo,
and the coyotes are howlin' like a choir.
Stars are shinin' bright, that north wind's cold tonight,
it's time to go gather 'round the fire.

We are the voice of the sagebrush congregation,
the long forgotten natives of the west.
More innocent tribes folk and wild country rascals
out here lookin' for peace and the rest.

We're the ancients of tomorrow,
we're the future of today,
mere young bloods from Tombstone,
please don't waste the living world away.

First rain on the dry ground, what a fragrance,
reminds me sure of when I was a boy,
playin' in the trees and scuffin' up my knees,
it's time to prepare the feast of joy.

Silver moonlight kisses the arroyo,
and the coyotes are howlin' like a choir.
Stars are shinin' bright, that north wind's cold tonight,
it's time to go gather 'round the fire.

We are the voice of the sagebrush congregation,
the long forgotten natives of the west.
More innocent tribes folk and wild country rascals
out here lookin' for peace and the rest.

We're the ancients of tomorrow,
we're the future of today,
mere young bloods from Tombstone,
please don't waste the living world away.

Don't waste the living world away.
It's old, so old and we're so young today.

THIS IS JUST WHAT I'D DO

If I ran the railroads in these United States,
I'd make sure all the stations had polished brass gates
and gardens to walk through with long winding paths
and rooms to stay over with showers and baths.
There'd be a gymnasium where people could play
and a pool to go swimmin' in sometime ev'ry day
and a big hall for dancin' and some really good food to eat
and the price of a ticket, well, it just could not be beat.

The best in the west and all just for you,
yes, if I ran the railroads, this is just what I'd do.
This is just what I'd do. This is just what I'd do.

If I ran the classrooms in these United States,
I'd make sure all the students knew measures and weights
and somethin' 'bout science and somethin' 'bout art
and somethin' 'bout takin' an engine apart.
There'd be a symposium 'bout practical stuff,
all the things that come in handy when the goin' gets rough
'cause there's so much more to life that just gawkin' at a screen
watchin' talkin' pictures hawkin' some new, slick, commercial scene.

The best in the west and all just for you,
yes, if I ran the classrooms, this is just what I'd do.
This is just what I'd do. This is just what I'd do.

If I ran the White House in these United States,
I'd make sure all the people could master their fates.
We'd clean up the country from ocean to ocean
and kick off a campaign of positive motion.
There'd be a moratorium on hunger and war
and we'd all work to build upon a solid ground floor.
We'd express to the world truth and goodness and beauty
and a sense of aesthetics and of conscientious duty.

The best in the west and all just for you,
yes, if I ran the White House, this is just what I'd do.
This is just what I'd do. This is just what I'd do.

WE'LL SPIN CARTWHEELS AROUND THE SUN

There's more to life than money, money, money.
There's more to life than power.
If we're gonna taste the honey, honey, honey,
we've got to find the flower,
find the flower.

We can't depend on that old, broken-down dream,
the handle's comin' off and there's a hole in the seam.
We can face the long, haunting shadows, face our phantoms and our fears;
see the end of the legions of empires; find our way to the River of Tears.

In the deep, deep dark of the deepest, darkest time,
deep inside great nature's seed stirs a living treasure trove;
soon to sprout, soon to climb, soon to poke up through the rime,
soon to bloom in ev'ry field from the mountain to the cove.

They say that mighty storm that's comin'
could swamp us all, drown ev'ryone,
but, if we make it through the maelstrom,
we'll spin cartwheels around the sun, cartwheels around the sun.

The air's so dirty, hard to see through the mire.
Some water, so polluted, it could spark and catch fire.
That old war machine, it's a monster made right here in our hometown.
Folks from ev'rywhere say they're against it, but the dark money's shouting them down.

Life's a hard, hard school, gettin' harder everyday,
hard for ev'ry living thing, ev'ry father, mother, child.
Gonna work, gonna play, gonna try to find our way
in a world that can't be tamed, in a world forever wild.

They say that mighty storm that's comin'
could swamp us all, drown ev'ryone,
but, if we make it through the maelstrom,
we'll spin cartwheels around the sun, cartwheels around the sun.

THE TRIBES

I've seen tribes gather in peace and in war,
I've seen them gather together before.
Oh, the tribes, they have gathered before.
The tribes have gathered before.
The tribes have gathered before.
The tribes, they have gathered before.

Now, Turtle Island's tangled in a trance,
startled by the silence of the spring.
This time, ev'ry brave must dance.
This time, ev'ry scout must sing.

For centuries untold 'til not so long ago
these rivers teemed with fishes, great and small.
The sky was full of birds, the land, with buffalo,
while ancient, wildwood forests towered tall.

Oh, this time, this time, too, will pass.
This time, this time, too, will pass.

In Alexander's time, Persia's kingdom fell,
a mighty man was he with such a tale to tell.
Oh, the tribes, they have gathered before.
The tribes have gathered before.
The tribes have gathered before.
The tribes, they have gathered before.

No more to war with painted shield and lance.
All 'round the spirit fire, let's form a ring.
This time, ev'ry brave must dance.
This time, ev'ry scout must sing.

Young Alexander's gone and Julius Caesar, too,
gone on to the graveyard of the gods.
Not Genghis Khan, Napoleon, not Hitler, me nor you,
can rule the world with magic rings and rods.

Oh, this time, this time, too, will pass.
This time, this time, too, will pass.

Yes! Now is the hour, climate change is real!
No time to dilly-dally, no time to spin the wheel.
Oh, the tribes, they have gathered before.
The tribes have gathered before.
The tribes have gathered before.
The tribes, they have gathered before.

We'll stand as one 'gainst greed's grotesque advance,
thwart autocrats and rogues who would be king.
This time, ev'ry brave must dance.
This time, ev'ry scout must sing.

Catch old 'Smooth-Moves' Machiavelli do his two-step on the telly,
twistin' truth up like a pretzel on the fly.
Ne'er undermined nor over ridden, the truth will not stay hidden
as it outshines ev'ry falsehood, ev'ry lie.

Oh, this time, this time, too, will pass.
This time, this time, too, will pass.

Since Pandora's jar of secrets came to haunt the universe,
the specter of atomic war looms, now, like an endless curse.
Oh, the tribes, they have gathered before.
The tribes have gathered before.
The tribes have gathered before.
The tribes, they have gathered before.

It's a dire, existential circumstance.
We've got to get a handle on the thing.
This time, ev'ry brave must dance.
This time, ev'ry scout must sing.

I've heard the distant thunder of the blazing outlaw guns
ripping through the empire's 'lectric eyes.
I've listened, too, with wonder, to a blessed choir of nuns
as they sang to me of life beyond the skies.

Oh, this time, this time, too, will pass.
This time, this time, too, will pass.

I know one day this dream I have will outrun these old bones,
'til then, I'll keep my vigil, brew my tea and set my stones.
Oh, the tribes, they have gathered before.
The tribes have gathered before.
The tribes have gathered before.
The tribes, they have gathered before.

I'll meet my sweet Geranium in France,
find a tree and make my love a swing.
And, all around the tree of life, we'll dance;
all around the tree of life, we'll sing.

All ye movers, all ye shakers, midnight trollers, kings of tweet,
there's a perfect storm a-stirrin', sakes alive!
In the maelstrom, folks are spinnin', swirlin', whirlin' down the street,
sayin': 'Got to pull together to survive!'

Oh, this time, this time, too, will pass.
This time, this time, too, will pass.

I've seen tribes gather in peace and in war,
I've seen them gather together before.
Oh, the tribes, they have gathered before.
The tribes have gathered before.
The tribes have gathered before.
The tribes, they have gathered before.

STARDUST HIGHWAY

*Took a walk one summer night
down stardust highway,
saw so many stars so bright
light up the skyway...*

*They say a day in never-never land
can last forever,
guess I'll be back from wonderland
the twelfth of never.*

*Universe expanding fast,
dreamers show us how it can.
Ev'ryone's wishin' on a star.*

*Truth and beauty, goodness knows,
lovers are your biggest fan.
Ev'ryone's wishin' on a star...in the night of wonder.*

*Ev'ryone is wishin' on one.
Ev'ryone knows deep down inside they are one.
Ev'ryone's wishin' on a star.*

*Standing on a bridge,
one end is anchored in stardust,
the other in starlight.*

*Starlight that spins, stardust that falls,
starlight that kisses these stardusted walls, that's all we are...
stardust in starlight, stardust in starlight, that's all.*

*Took a walk one summer night
down stardust highway,
saw so many stars so bright
light up the skyway...*

BIG TIME WORLD OF LOVE

Gonna rendezvous at the waterfall,
gonna swim in the sparklin' pools;
drink that fresh lemonade at high noon;
dance all night with the fun lovin' fools.

Bring down your good friend Christina
and Mary and Sarah and Jane
and the tall, Macedonian sculptor
and Kidd Alabaster and Shane.

And you will be happy, you will find release,
laughin' in the moonlight, fallin' in the fleece.
And you will be singin' and dancin' in the streets,
makin' love on the mountain while the jungle bird tweets.

Come into the love-world,
the big time world of love, love, love, love.
Come into the love-world,
big time world of love, yeah, love, yeah,
love, yeah, love, yeah . . .

Gonna rise with the sun in the morning,
gonna work in the fields all day long;
rest in the still of the evening,
'til the angel of sleep sings her song.

Gonna breathe in the fragrance of jasmine;
gonna dream 'til the night rolls away
while the wind blows the scent of sweet cinnamon
by the place in the hills where we lay.

And you will be happy, you will find release,
laughin' in the moonlight, fallin' in the fleece.
And you will be singin' and dancin' in the streets,
makin' love on the mountain while the jungle bird tweets.

Come into the love-world,
the big time world of love, love, love, love.
Come into the love-world,
big time world of love, yeah, love, yeah,
love, yeah, love, yeah . . .

WE PULLED TOGETHER

It hadn't rained for ages, but we weren't standin' still.
We dug a hard rock cistern, tapped the springs on yonder hill.
Through summer's heat, through wind and dust, we toiled with naught but will
and when the rains came pourin' down, we danced and drank our fill.

The vagabonds were hungry and in an awful mood.
We rustled up some nourishment and brought them all some food.
The ruckus, it died down a bit, the frenzy was subdued.
Amazing how some sustenance can change an attitude.

We pulled together, that is what we did.
We pulled together, fore and aft and mid.
Sometimes we'd slip, sometimes we'd fall,
sometimes we'd take the skid,
but, we pulled together,
that is what we did.

The fire in the infirmary, we never will forget.
No one knew the source of it, nor why the blaze was set.
Ev'ryone escaped the flames, but, we weren't finished yet.
We searched and found the scoundrels, now, they're bound to their regret.

Down at McGillicuddy's amidst the happy throng,
we raised a glass to all that's right and ev'rything that's wrong.
We asked old man O'Callaghan how he had lived so long?
"I rise up with the sun", he said, "and end the day with song".

We pulled together, that is what we did.
We pulled together, fore and aft and mid.
Sometimes we'd slip, sometimes we'd fall,
sometimes we'd take the skid,
but, we pulled together,
that is what we did.

MUSIC IS WRITTEN IN NATURE'S EQUILIBRIUM

Music is written in nature's equilibrium
whose subtle universe is the garden of all flowers, of all perfections.

As foot falls dancing on labyrinthine paths
and cool evening rains sprinkle down,
let me scoop up rich earth in my hands
sensing in its aromatic mixture
consummate plays of matter.

This is the ground that grows ten-thousand multiplicities.
This is the densest of rays falling out from space.
This is the element of supreme desire.
This is the beauty of Earth.

SPACE SINGS

*Space sings
e'vry atom's galaxy
humming motion's grand illusion
through the house of heaven's stars.
Passing songs beyond Polaris,
shining brightly in the suns.
Eclipsed by planets revolutions,
cooled in phasing moonlight orbits.
Spun through water's coursing streams,
amid the scent of Earth's bouquet,
beyond the forms of fiery things
and atmospheres that dance in rings,
space sings.*

PAEAN TO THE JESTER'S CROWN

*In remembrance of the Scottish lad, the poet, Robert Burns -
here's to the timeless songs he penned and here's to Auld Lang Syne.*

*As Winter's season rushes in
and old Jack Frost drops by,
may love and joy and peace be yours
as Solstice day draws nigh.*

*Humor is the Jester's crown,
whose wit makes angels sing.
Long may your jovial spirit thrive,
long may your laughter ring.*

A CITIZEN'S PLEDGE

*I pledge allegiance to the truth
and to the beauty for which it stands,
one spirit, indivisible, with goodness and mercy for all.*

*For access to other work created by the author,
visit the following websites:*

Amazon: DIGA Tapestry:
https://www.amazon.com/Fine-Art-Tapestries-Finished-European/dp/B07CZGNZ9V/ref=pd_ybh_a_42?_encoding=UTF8&psc=1&refRID=J4TKB4W8WZFGAGJW68VJ

A Woven Tapestry / Artwork by Jordan De La Sierra
http://www.finearttapestries.com/diga-wall-tapestry/

Jordan De La Sierra: Gymnosphere: Song of the Rose
Music for the Well-Tuned Piano – Recorded in 1976 – Complete
https://www.youtube.com/watch?v=iGjmGBtYZl8

Amazon: Song of the Rose / CD
https://www.amazon.com/dp/B00OC7MEII/ref=dm_rwp_pur_lnd_albm_unrg

Jordan De La Sierra: Soft Spin / Valentine Eleven
https://soundcloud.com/jordandelasierra/soft-spin

Jordan De La Sierra: Hymn to the World Indian / Valentine Eleven
https://soundcloud.com/jordandelasierra/hymn-to-the-world-indian?in=jordandelasierra/sets/valentine-eleven

Jordan De La Sierra: Long-Distance Messenger / Valentine Eleven
https://soundcloud.com/jordandelasierra/long-distance-messenger

Jordan De La Sierra: Nimbu-Pani: The Lemon -Water Song / Valentine Eleven
https://soundcloud.com/jordandelasierra/nimbu-pani-the-lemon-water

Jordan De La Sierra: Valentine Eleven – Complete
https://fromthestacks.bandcamp.com/album/valentine-eleven

www.ingramcontent.com/pod-product-compliance
Lightning Source LLC
LaVergne TN
LVHW070215080526
838202LV00067B/6822